ExpressWays

Second Edition

2

Steven J. Molinsky
Bill Bliss

Contributing Author
Ann Kennedy

PRENTICE HALL REGENTS
A VIACOM COMPANY
Upper Saddle River, NJ 07458

Molinsky, Steven J.
ExpressWays 2 / Steven J. Molinsky, Bill Bliss, – – 2nd ed.
  p.   cm.
Includes index.
ISBN 0-13-385337-3. (soft cover: alk. paper)
  1. English language– –Textbooks for foreign speakers.   I. Bliss,
Bill. II. Title..
PE1128.M6753   1995
428.2'4– –dc20

95-44120
CIP

Publisher: *Tina Carver*
Director of Production: *Aliza Greenblatt*
Editorial Production/Design Manager: *Dominick Mosco*
Production Supervision/Compositor: *Janice Sivertsen*
Production Editors/Compositors: *Don Kilcoyne/Ken Liao/Christine Mann*
Editorial Supervision: *Janet Johnston*
Production Assistant: *Jennifer Rella*
Manufacturing Manager: *Ray Keating*

Electronic Art Production Supervision: *Todd Ware*
Electronic Art Production/Scanning: *Marita Froimson*
Electronic Art: *Marita Froimson/Don Kilcoyne/Jan Sivertsen/Ken Liao*
Art Director: *Merle Krumper*
Interior Design: *PC&F and Wanda España*
Photographer: *Paul Tañedo*

Illustrator: *Richard Hill*

PRENTICE HALL REGENTS
A VIACOM COMPANY

© 1996 by PRENTICE HALL REGENTS
Prentice-Hall, Inc.
A Simon & Schuster Company
Upper Saddle River, New Jersey 07458

10   9   8   7   6

ISBN 0-13-385337-3 •

Prentice-Hall International (UK) Limited, *London*
Prentice-Hall of Australia Pty. Limited, *Sydney*
Prentice-Hall Canada Inc., *Toronto*
Prentice-Hall Hispanoamericana, S.A., *Mexico*
Prentice-Hall of India Private Limited, *New Delhi*
Prentice-Hall of Japan, Inc., *Tokyo*
Simon & Schuster Asia Pte. Ltd., *Singapore*
Editora Prentice-Hall do Brasil, Ltda., *Rio de Janeiro*

EXPRESSWAYS 2 TRAVEL GUIDE

EXIT 3 • Food 43

iv

EXIT 6 • Rules and Regulations — 105

EXIT 7 • School, Family, and Friends — 127

ExpressWays is a comprehensive 4-level course for learners of English. Its innovative spiraled curriculum integrates lifeskill topics, functions, and grammar in an imaginative highway theme that puts students *in the fast lane* for an exciting and motivating journey to English language proficiency.

The program consists of the following components:

- **Student Texts** — offering speaking, reading, writing, and listening comprehension practice that integrates grammar and functions in a topic-based curriculum.

- **Activity Workbooks** — offering reinforcement through grammar, reading, writing, and listening comprehension practice fully coordinated with the student texts. The activity workbooks also feature dynamic exercises in pronunciation, rhythm, stress, and intonation.

- *Navigator* **Companion Books** — visually exciting "magazine-style" texts, offering a complete lifeskill curriculum fully integrated with the *ExpressWays* student texts.

- **Teacher's Guides** — providing background notes and expansion activities for all lessons and step-by-step instructions for teachers.

- **Audio Program** — offering realistic presentations of conversations, listening comprehension exercises, and readings from the student texts and workbooks.

- **Picture Program** — featuring Picture Cards for vocabulary development, enrichment exercises, and role-playing activities.

- **Placement and Achievement Testing Program** — providing tools for the evaluation of student levels and progress.

The *ExpressWays* series is organized by a spiraled curriculum that is covered at different degrees of intensity and depth at each level. *ExpressWays 1* and *2* provide beginning-level students with the most important vocabulary, grammar, and functional expressions needed to communicate at a basic level in a full range of situations and contexts. *ExpressWays 3* and *4* cover the same full range of situations and contexts, but offer intermediate-level students expanded vocabulary, more complex grammar, and a wider choice of functional expressions.

The Dimensions of Communication: Function, Form, and Content

ExpressWays provides dynamic, communicative practice that involves students in lively interactions based on the content of real-life contexts and situations. Every lesson offers students simultaneous practice with one or more functions, the grammatical forms needed to express those functions competently, and the contexts and situations in which the functions and grammar are used. This "tri-dimensional" clustering of function, form, and content is the organizing principle behind each lesson and the cornerstone of the *ExpressWays* approach to functional syllabus design.

ExpressWays offers students broad exposure to uses of language in a variety of relevant contexts: in community, school, employment, home, and social settings. The series gives students practice using a variety of registers, from the formal language someone might use in a job interview, with a customer, or when speaking to an authority figure, to the informal language someone would use when talking with family members, co-workers, or friends.

A special feature of the course is the treatment of discourse strategies — initiating conversations and topics, hesitating, asking for clarification, and other conversation skills.

An Overview

Chapter-Opening Photos

Each chapter-opening page features two photographs of situations that depict key topics presented in the chapter. Students make predictions about who the people are and what they might be saying to each other. In this way, students have the opportunity to share what they already know and to relate the chapter's content to their own lives and experiences.

Guided Conversations

Guided conversations are the dialogs and exercises that are the central learning devices in *ExpressWays*. Each lesson begins with a model conversation that depicts a real-life situation and the vocabulary, grammar, and functions used in the communication exchange. In the exercises that follow, students create new conversations by placing new content into the framework of the model.

Original Student Conversations

Each lesson ends with an open-ended exercise that offers students the opportunity to create and present original conversations based on the theme of the lesson. Students contribute content based on their experiences, ideas, and imaginations.

Follow-Up Exercises and Activities

A variety of follow-up exercises and activities reinforce and build upon the topics, functions, and grammar presented in the guided conversation lessons.

- **Constructions Ahead!** exercises provide focused practice with grammar structures.

- **CrossTalk** activities provide opportunities for students to relate lesson content to their own lives.

- **InterActions** activities provide opportunities for role-playing and cooperative learning.

- **Interview** activities encourage students to interview each other as well as people in the community.

- **Community Connections** activities provide task-based homework for students to get out into their communities to practice their language skills.

- **Cultural Intersections** activities offer rich opportunities for cross-cultural comparison.

- **Figure It Out!** activities offer opportunities for problem-solving.

- **Your Turn** activities provide opportunities for writing and discussion of issues presented in the chapter.

- **Listening Exercises** give students intensive listening practice that focuses on functional communication.

- **Reflections** activities provide frequent opportunities for self-assessment, critical thinking, and problem-solving.

- **Reading** passages in every chapter are designed to provide interesting and stimulating content for class discussion. These selections are also available on the accompanying audiotapes for additional listening comprehension practice.

InterChange

This end-of-chapter activity offers students the opportunity to create and present "guided role plays." Each activity consists of a model that students can practice and then use as a basis for their original presentations. Students should be encouraged to be inventive and to use new vocabulary in these presentations and should feel free to adapt and expand the model any way they wish.

Rest Stop

These "free role plays" appear after every few chapters, offering review and synthesis of the topics, functions, and grammar of the preceding chapters. Students are presented with eight scenes depicting conversations between people in various situations. The students determine who the people are and what they are talking about, and then improvise based on their perceptions of the scenes' characters, contexts, and situations. These improvisations promote students' absorption of the preceding chapters' functions and grammar into their repertoire of active language use.

Support and Reference Sections

End-of-Chapter Summaries include the following:

- **Looking Back** — a listing of key vocabulary in the chapter for review.

- **Construction Sign** — a listing of the key grammar structures presented in the chapter.

- **ExpressWays Checklist** — a self-assessment listing of key lifeskills presented in the chapter.

An **Appendix** provides charts of the grammar constructions presented in each chapter, along with a list of cardinal numbers, ordinal numbers, and irregular verbs.

An **Index** provides a convenient reference for locating topics and grammar in the text.

Suggested Teaching Strategies

We encourage you, in using *ExpressWays*, to develop approaches and strategies that are compatible with your own teaching syle and the needs and abilities of your students. While the program does not require any specific method or technique in order to be used effectively, you may find it helpful to review and try out some of the following suggestions. (Specific step-by-step instructions may be found in the *ExpressWays* Teacher's Guides.)

Chapter-Opening Photos

Have students talk about the people and the situations and, as a class or in pairs, predict what the characters might be saying to each other. Students in pairs or small groups may enjoy practicing role plays based on these scenes and then presenting them to the class.

Guided Conversations

1. SETTING THE SCENE: Have students look at the model illustration in the book. Set the scene: Who are the people? What is the situation?

2. LISTENING: With books closed, have students listen to the model conversation — presented by you, by a pair of students, or on the audiotape.

3. CLASS PRACTICE: With books still closed, model each line and have the whole class practice in unison.

4. READING: With books open, have students follow along as two students present the model.

5. PAIR PRACTICE: In pairs, have students practice the model conversation.

6. EXERCISE PRACTICE: (optional) Have pairs of students simultaneously practice all the exercises.

7. EXERCISE PRESENTATIONS: Call on pairs of students to present the exercises.

Original Student Conversations

In these activities, which follow the guided conversations at the end of each lesson, have students create and present original conversations based on the theme of the lesson. Encourage students to be inventive as they create their characters and situations. (You may ask students to prepare their original conversations as homework, then practice them the next day with another student and present them to the class. In this way, students can review the previous day's lesson without actually having to repeat the specific exercises already covered.)

CrossTalk

Have students first work in pairs and then share with the class what they talked about.

InterActions

Have pairs of students practice role playing the activity and then present their role plays to the class.

InterView

Have students circulate around the room to conduct their interviews, or have students interview people outside the class. Students should then report to the class about their interviews.

Community Connections

Have students do the activity individually, in pairs, or in small groups and then report to the class.

Cultural Intersections

Have students do the activity as a class, in pairs, or in small groups.

Reflections

Have students discuss the questions in pairs or small groups, and then share their ideas with the class.

Your Turn

This activity is designed for both writing practice and discussion. Have students discuss the activity as a class, in pairs, or in small groups. Then have students write their responses at home, share their written work with other students, and discuss in class. Students may enjoy keeping a journal of their written work. If time permits, you may want to write a response to each student's journal, sharing your own opinions and experiences as well as reacting to what the student has written. If you are keeping portfolios of students' work, these compositions serve as excellent examples of students' progress in learning English.

Reading

Have students discuss the topic of the reading beforehand, using the pre-reading questions suggested in the Teacher's Guide. Have students then read the passage silently, or have them listen to the passage and take notes as you read it or play the audiotape.

InterChange

Have students practice the model, using the same steps listed above for guided conversations. Then have pairs of students create and present original conversations, using the model dialog as a guide. Encourage students to be inventive and to use new vocabulary. (You may want to assign this exercise as homework, having students prepare their conversations, practice them the next day with another student, and then present them to the class.) Students should present their conversations without referring to the written text, but they should also not memorize them. Rather, they should feel free to adapt and expand them any way they wish.

Rest Stop

Have students talk about the people and the situations, and then present role plays based on the scenes. Students may refer back to previous lessons as a resource, but they should not simply re-use specific conversations. (You may want to assign these exercises as written homework, having students prepare their conversations, practice them the next day with another student, and then present them to the class.)

We hope that *ExpressWays* offers you and your students a journey to English that is meaningful, effective, and entertaining. Have a nice trip!

Steven J. Molinsky
Bill Bliss

ExpressWays

Second Edition

2

Exit 1

FRIENDS AND NEIGHBORS

Take Exit 1 to . . .

- Greet someone and introduce yourself, using *wh-questions*
- Ask information about a neighborhood, using *wh-questions* and *yes/no questions*
- Ask permission to do something, using *can*
- Offer to help someone, using two-word verbs
- Ask a favor of someone
- Tell about things you did, using the past tense
- Give advice to someone, using *should*
- Call about a housing problem

Functions This Exit!

Asking for and Reporting Information
Greeting People
Offering to Help Someone
Gratitude
Appreciation
Checking and Indicating Understanding
Initiating a Topic
Permission
Requests
Advice–Suggestions

Karen is a new neighbor in Peter's apartment building. What do you think these two neighbors are saying to each other?

Victor is having problems with his kitchen sink. What do you think he and his friend Eric are saying to each other?

A. Hello. I'm your neighbor. My name is Helen.

B. Hi. I'm Maria. Nice to meet you.

A. Nice meeting you, too. Tell me, where are you from?

B. Mexico. And you?

A. Greece.

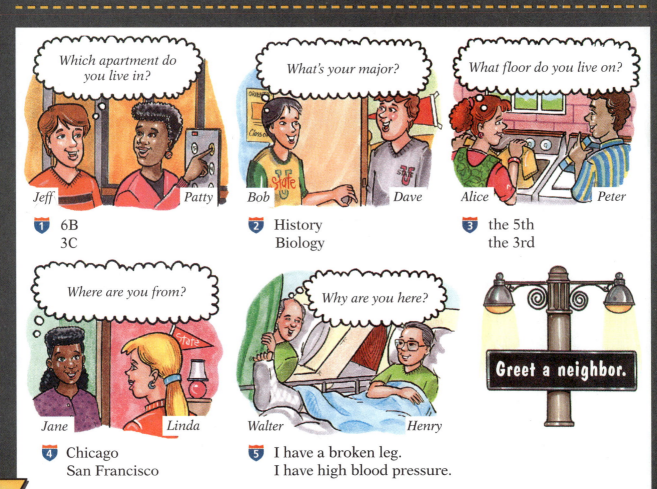

1. 6B
   3C

2. History
   Biology

3. the 5th
   the 3rd

4. Chicago
   San Francisco

5. I have a broken leg.
   I have high blood pressure.

Greet a neighbor.

Fill It In!

Fill in the correct WH-word.

| Who | What | Where | When | Why | Which | How |

1. _Where_ are you from?   Japan.
2. _____ apartment do you live in?   Apartment 302.
3. _____ are you going?   To the airport.
4. _____ is Peter in the hospital?   He had a heart attack.
5. _____ is going to baby-sit?   Patty.
6. _____ did you start your new job?   On Monday.
7. _____ did Hector study?   History.
8. _____ are you?   Fine. And you?
9. _____ can't you go to the movies with us?   I have to do my English homework.

Matching Lines

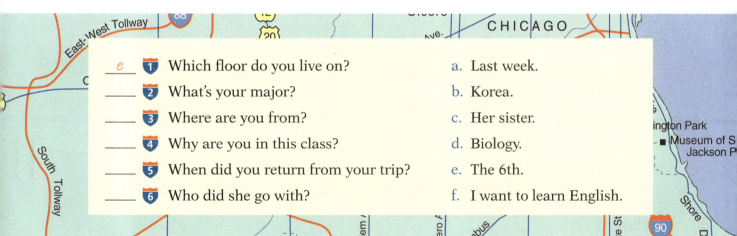

_e_ 1	Which floor do you live on?	a. Last week.
___ 2	What's your major?	b. Korea.
___ 3	Where are you from?	c. Her sister.
___ 4	Why are you in this class?	d. Biology.
___ 5	When did you return from your trip?	e. The 6th.
___ 6	Who did she go with?	f. I want to learn English.

CrossTalk

Talk with a partner about your neighbors.

What are their names?
How often do you see them?
What do you talk about?

Report to the class about your discussion.

REFLECTIONS
When you meet a person for the first time, what questions do you ask? What do you talk about?

Discuss in pairs or small groups, and then share your ideas with the class.

3

A. Excuse me. I'm new here. Can I ask you a question?

B. Sure.

A. Is there a laundromat in the neighborhood?

B. Yes. There's a laundromat around the corner.

A. Around the corner?

B. Yes.

A. Thanks very much.

Ask about a new neighborhood.

Fill It In!

Fill in the correct word.

Does	•	Do	Is	•	Are

1 ___Do___ they pick up the garbage today?

2 _____ you going to the laundromat?

3 _____ the superintendent live in the building?

4 _____ you drive to work every day?

5 _____ there many children in the neighborhood?

6 _____ the mail come on Saturdays?

7 _____ your friends live in the building?

8 _____ the apartment on the 10th floor vacant?

9 _____ it hot in your apartment?

10 _____ you happy in your neighborhood?

Listen

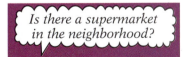

Listen and choose the correct answer.

1 a. Certainly.
b. What's your name?

2 a. Yes, I do.
b. On the 3rd floor.

3 a. No.
b. On the 1st floor.

4 a. Actually, yes.
b. At a restaurant.

5 a. At 10:00.
b. On Pine Street.

6 a. On the 2nd floor.
b. No. He lives in the basement.

7 a. No. It's hot.
b. Yes. Down the block.

8 a. About thirty.
b. Yes, there are.

9 a. Today.
b. At about 8:00.

InterActions

You're moving into a new apartment building. You meet a new neighbor and ask a lot of questions about the neighborhood. For example:

Is there a bus stop nearby?

What time does the mail come?

Is there a supermarket in the neighborhood?

What other questions do you have, and what does your neighbor tell you? Role-play with a partner and then present your "neighborly" conversations to the class.

Your Turn

For Writing and Discussion

Tell about the neighborhood where YOU live. What are the advantages of living there?

A. Pardon me. Can I ask you a question?

B. Certainly.

A. Can I park my car here?

B. Yes, you can.

A. Thanks.

A. Pardon me. Can I ask you a question?

B. Certainly.

A. Can I use my fireplace?

B. No, you can't.

A. Oh, okay. Thanks.

Ask permission to do something in an apartment building.

ExpressWays

Can I _____?
Yes, you can.
No, you can't.

1 Can I leave my bike here?   Yes, _you can_ .

2 Can my friends park in front of the building?   No, _____.

3 Can we hang our laundry on the balcony?   Yes, _____.

4 Can Mrs. King plant a garden in the backyard?   No, _____.

5 Can my brother and I play here?   Yes, _____.

6 Can I use the fireplace?   No, _____.

Fill It In!

Fill in the correct word.

1 You can't hang your _____ here.
    a. garbage
    (b.) laundry

2 My wife is going to plant a _____.
    a. garden
    b. building

3 Go down the block to the _____.
    a. basement
    b. bus stop

4 They _____ the garbage today.
    a. deliver
    b. pick up

5 The _____ comes at about noon.
    a. mail
    b. bus stop

6 The _____ can't come now.
    a. supermarket
    b. superintendent

InterActions

You're the superintendent of an apartment building. Decide on the rules of your building — what things the tenants **can** and **can't** do in the building. Make a list.

Another student in the class is a new tenant and asks you all about the rules of the building.

Present your conversations to the class and compare the rules and regulations in each other's apartment buildings.

REFLECTIONS
Why are rules and regulations important?

Discuss in pairs or small groups, and then share your ideas with the class.

Can I Help You Take Out the Garbage?

take out the garbage

pick up your things

A. Can I help you take out the garbage?

B. No. That's okay. I can take it out myself.

A. Please. Let me help you.

B. Well, all right. If you don't mind.

A. No, not at all.

B. Thanks. I appreciate it.

A. Can I help you pick up your things?

B. No. That's okay. I can pick them up myself.

A. Please. Let me help you.

B. Well, all right. If you don't mind.

A. No, not at all.

B. Thanks. I appreciate it.

1 hang up your laundry

2 put away these chairs

3 carry those bags

4 cut down that tree

5 clean up this mess

Offer to help a neighbor.

Constructions Ahead!

put away – put it away	hang up – hang it up
take out – take it out	pick up – pick it up
cut down – cut it down	clean up – clean it up

it   them

1 Did you pick __up__ your package at the post office?

Yes. I _picked_ __it__ __up__ yesterday.

2 Can I help you cut _____ those trees over there?

Sure. We can _____ _____ _____ together.

3 Can I hang _____ my laundry on the balcony?

No, but you can _____ _____ _____ in back of the building.

4 Did your son take _____ the garbage?

Yes. He _____ _____ _____ this morning.

5 Can you put _____ these tables and chairs?

Yes. I can _____ _____ _____ right now.

6 Clean _____ this mess right now!

Okay. But I can't _____ _____ _____ myself!

7 Please pick _____ those heavy bags for me.

I can't. Please ask Michael to _____ _____ _____.

8 You should hang _____ your suits.

I'm going to _____ _____ _____ right now.

9 I have to put _____ the plates and glasses.

Here. I can help you _____ _____ _____.

Figure It Out!

You're doing a household chore, and you obviously need some help! Pantomime the activity and see if other students in the class can figure out what you're doing and offer to help you.

> *I see you're _____ing.*
> *Can I help you _____ _____ _____?*

CrossTalk

Talk with a partner about your neighbors. Are they friendly? Are they helpful? Tell about a time you helped a neighbor. Tell about a time a neighbor helped you.

9

Could You Lend Me a Hammer?

lend me a hammer

A. Could I ask you a favor?

B. What is it?

A. Could you lend me a hammer?

B. All right.

A. Are you sure?

B. Yes. I'd be happy to lend you a hammer.

A. Thanks. I appreciate it.

1 help me start my car

2 lend me some flour

3 help me with my shopping bags

4 take care of Billy for a few minutes

5 pick up my mail while I'm away

Ask a favor of someone.

Constructions Ahead!

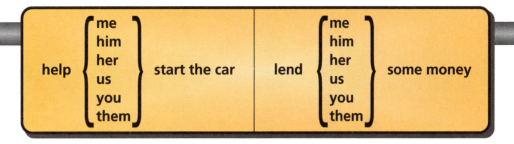

| help | me
him
her
us
you
them | start the car | lend | me
him
her
us
you
them | some money |

1. I'd like to pick up this mess. Can you help _me_ pick it up?

2. Richard wants to fix the shelves. Let's lend _____ our hammer.

3. Kathy and Susan are making a cake. Can you give _____ some eggs?

4. Alice can't find her purse. Can you lend _____ some money?

5. Tim and Bob can't carry those boxes. Let's help _____ take the boxes up to the sixth floor.

6. My roommate and I don't have a car. Can you possibly lend _____ your car tonight?

7. Please write me a letter. Let me give _____ my address.

8. It's my sister's birthday tomorrow. I'm going to give _____ flowers for her birthday.

9. This Sunday is Harold and Gertrude's anniversary. Let's send _____ flowers.

10. Everybody in our family loves to listen to Uncle Charlie. He always tells _____ wonderful stories about his exciting life.

11. This English homework is very difficult. Can you please help _____ with it?

Survey

Ask favors of some people you know. For example:

> *Can you lend me _____?*

> *Can you possibly help me _____?*

> *Could you please give me _____?*

What do they say? Do they help you? Report your findings to the class and compare everybody's experiences.

11

A. You know, I knocked on your door several times last week, but you weren't home.

B. No, I wasn't. I was in Detroit.

A. Oh. What did you do there?

B. I visited my daughter and her husband.

A. Oh. That's nice.

12

*come–came
ring–rang

Fill It In!

Fill in the correct word.

did • didn't   was   wasn't   were • weren't

1 ___Did___ you clean up that mess yet? No, I _didn't_ . I _was_ busy all morning.

2 Where _____ you yesterday afternoon? I took my son to the doctor. He _____ feel well.

3 _____ you call me this morning? No, I _____. I _____ home. I _____ at school.

4 I stopped by your house last night, but you _____ there. That's right. I _____. My husband and I _____ at a meeting.

5 What _____ you do over the weekend? Nothing special. I _____ home alone all weekend.

6 Where _____ Maria yesterday? I _____ see her in class. I _____. She _____ in the back of the room.

came • went   saw   drove   took   rang   had   read • heard

7 Where did you go? We ___went___ to the zoo.

8 When did you take the garbage out? I _____ it out this morning.

9 What did they see at the movies? They _____ a very funny comedy.

10 Did you hear something? Yes. Somebody _____ the doorbell.

11 Why were you late? Jim and I _____ to clean up.

12 Do you want the newspaper? No, thanks. I _____ it already.

13 When were Jose and Carlos here? They _____ by about an hour ago.

14 How did Mrs. Kitano get to the beach? She _____.

15 How did you find out about the big storm? I _____ about it on the radio.

16 When did Herbert go to the airport? He _____ at about 6:00.

Your Turn

For Writing and Discussion

Many of the people on page 12 went on trips to some exciting places. Tell about a place YOU visited. Where did you go? When? What did you do there?

A. What are you doing?

B. I'm trying to fix my kitchen sink.

A. What's wrong with it?

B. It's leaking.

A. I see. And you're trying to fix it yourself?

B. Yes. But I'm having a lot of trouble.

A. You know, maybe you should call a plumber.

B. Hmm. You're probably right.

1 call an electrician

2 call a carpenter

3 call the gas company

4 call the superintendent

5 call a plumber

Give a neighbor some helpful advice.

14

ExpressWays

| an electrician ○ a carpenter | a plumber | the superintendent ○ the gas company |

1 My basement door doesn't close!   Call _a carpenter_.

2 The light switch in my bedroom doesn't work!   Call _____.

3 My oven doesn't go on!   Call _____.

4 My toilet doesn't flush!   Call _____.

5 The heat in our apartment isn't working!   Call _____.

Listen

Listen and write the number next to the correct picture.

_____   _____   1

_____   _____

Community Connections

As a class, compile a list of people to call in case of emergencies. Write down the names and phone numbers of plumbers, electricians, carpenters, the gas company, the telephone company repair service, and others you think are important to call. Publish this **Emergency Directory** and give a copy to each student in your class.

15

Do You Fix Kitchen Sinks?

A. Ace Plumbing Company.

B. Hello. Do you fix kitchen sinks?

A. Yes. What's the problem?

B. My kitchen sink is leaking.

A. I see. We can send a plumber at two o'clock this afternoon. Is that okay?

B. Two o'clock this afternoon? Yes, that's fine.

A. Okay. What's the name?

B. Eric Jensen.

A. Spell the last name, please.

B. J-E-N-S-E-N.

A. And the address?

B. 93 Cliff Street.

A. Phone number?

B. 972-3053.

A. All right. A plumber will be there at two o'clock this afternoon.

B. Thank you.

A. _____.

B. Hello. Do you fix _____s?

A. Yes. What's the problem?

B. _____.

A. I see. We can send a _____ at _____. Is that okay?

B. _____? Yes, that's fine.

A. Okay. What's the name?

B. _____.

A. Spell the last name, please.

B. _____.

A. And the address?

B. _____.

A. Phone number?

B. _____.

A. All right. A _____ will be there at _____.

B. Thank you.

Something in your home is broken. Call a plumber, a carpenter, or an electrician, using the model dialog above as a guide. Feel free to adapt and expand the model any way you wish.

Matching Lines

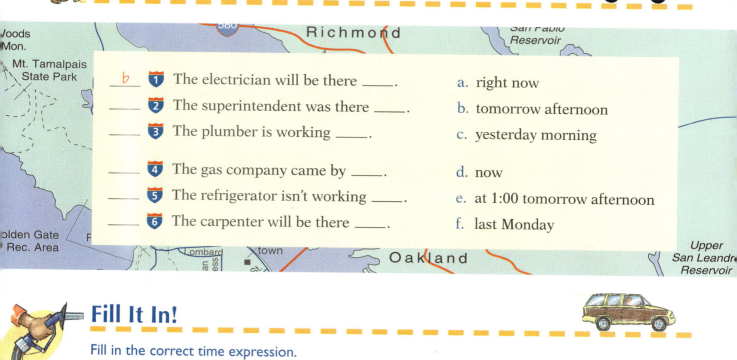

b [1] The electrician will be there ____.	a. right now
____ [2] The superintendent was there ____.	b. tomorrow afternoon
____ [3] The plumber is working ____.	c. yesterday morning
____ [4] The gas company came by ____.	d. now
____ [5] The refrigerator isn't working ____.	e. at 1:00 tomorrow afternoon
____ [6] The carpenter will be there ____.	f. last Monday

Fill It In!

Fill in the correct time expression.

[1] We can send an electrician at 4:00 _____ afternoon.
   (a.) tomorrow
   b. yesterday

[2] Can I help you _____ ?
   a. last Thursday
   b. this afternoon

[3] I called the gas company several times _____ .
   a. last Tuesday
   b. next Tuesday

[4] I called you. Where were you _____ ?
   a. tomorrow night
   b. yesterday evening

[5] David is arriving _____ .
   a. this evening
   b. yesterday afternoon

[6] I can help you make the beds _____ .
   a. a little while ago
   b. at about 10:00

[7] Clean up this mess _____ !
   a. last Sunday
   b. right now

[8] They did that _____ .
   a. already
   b. tomorrow

[9] Mrs. Brady fixed the kitchen sink _____ .
   a. tomorrow afternoon
   b. at around 3:00

[10] Mr. Chen had trouble with his car _____ .
   a. next week
   b. a little while ago

REFLECTIONS
How much does it cost when a plumber, a carpenter, or an electrician comes to your apartment or home? Do you think this is expensive? Why or why not?

Discuss in pairs or small groups, and then share your ideas with the class.

Listen

Listen and choose the correct response.

[1] (a.) Yes. What's the problem?
   b. Which electricians?

[2] a. On the first floor.
   b. The switches don't work.

[3] a. You're welcome.
   b. That's fine.

[4] a. Elaine Hall.
   b. In the bedrooms.

[5] a. 3 Pines Road.
   b. And a shirt.

[6] a. About fifteen.
   b. 227-4586.

Richard got* home from work at 7:30 yesterday evening. He took the elevator to his sixth-floor apartment. He opened the door and saw water on his floor! First, he went to the kitchen. The sink in the kitchen wasn't leaking. Then he checked the bathroom. The toilet wasn't leaking, and the bathroom sink wasn't leaking. Finally, he went into the living room and looked up at the ceiling. The light was leaking!

Richard ran* upstairs to the apartment above his on the seventh floor. He knocked on the door and rang the doorbell, but his neighbor, Mr. Martino, wasn't home. Richard went back to his apartment. He was worried. So he decided to call the superintendent of the building.

Mr. Tanaka, the superintendent, was very helpful. He went to Richard's apartment right away, and then he and Richard went upstairs to the seventh floor. Mr. Tanaka opened the door to Mr. Martino's apartment, and they saw the problem immediately. Mr. Martino's dishwasher was leaking! There was water everywhere! Mr. Tanaka turned off the dishwasher. Then he went downstairs and fixed the light in Richard's living room. He even helped Richard clean up the water on his floor.

Richard really appreciated Mr. Tanaka's help, so he invited Mr. Tanaka to have a cup of coffee. They sat* and talked all evening about life in the apartment building.

What Happened?

1 Why was Richard surprised when he got home from work yesterday?

2 Which of these *weren't* leaking?
(the kitchen sink / the bathroom sink / the living room light / the toilet)

3 Why did Richard call the superintendent?

4 What was the problem?

5 What did Mr. Tanaka do when he discovered the problem?

6 How did Richard and Mr. Tanaka celebrate their "victory"?

18

* get–got
  run–ran
  sit–sat

Do You Remember?

Try to answer these questions without looking back at the story on page 18.

1 There was water on Richard's _____ .
   a. apartment
   (b.) floor

2 The water was in the _____ .
   a. kitchen
   b. living room

3 Mr. Martino lives _____ .
   a. downstairs
   b. upstairs

4 Richard rang Mr. Martino's _____ .
   a. doorbell
   b. door

5 He also knocked on his _____ .
   a. doorbell
   b. door

6 Richard called the superintendent because he was _____ .
   a. leaking
   b. upset

7 Mr. Tanaka _____ in the building.
   a. works
   b. fixes

8 Mr. Tanaka first went to _____ .
   a. Mr. Martino's apartment
   b. Richard's apartment

9 The problem was with the _____ .
   a. dishwasher
   b. leaking

10 Mr. Tanaka _____ the dishwasher.
   a. turned on
   b. turned off

11 He also fixed Richard's _____ .
   a. light
   b. dishwasher

12 Richard invited Mr. Tanaka into his apartment because he wanted to _____ him.
   a. talk
   b. thank

InterActions

With a partner, create a reenactment of the story on page 18. Present your "dramas" to the class and compare the different versions of this emergency saga.

Your Turn

For Writing and Discussion

Tell about a time when you had an emergency at home.

What was the emergency?
Who did you call?
Did the person help you?
Was there any damage to your home?

Looking Back

- [ ] **Housing**
  apartment
  balcony
  basement
  building
  doorbell
  fireplace
  floor
  front door
  garbage
  garbage bags

  garden
  laundry
  neighbor
  superintendent

- [ ] **Community**
  bus stop
  laundromat
  mail
  supermarket

- [ ] **Household Fixtures and Appliances**
  kitchen sink
  light
  oven
  radiator
  stove
  toilet

- [ ] **Household Repairs**
  carpenter
  electrician
  gas company
  plumber

- [ ] **Personal Information**
  address
  last name
  name
  phone number

- [ ] **Family Members**
  cousin
  daughter
  grandchildren
  husband
  son

Now Leaving Exit 1 Construction Area

- [ ] **Review:**
  To Be: Present Tense
  Simple Present Tense
  WH-Questions
  Object Pronouns
  Should
  To Be: Past Tense
  Simple Past Tense
  Yes/No Questions
  Can
- [ ] **Two-Word Verbs**
- [ ] **Time Expressions**

Sorry for the inconvenience. For more information see pages 168–169.

ExpressWays Checklist

I can . . .
- [ ] greet someone and introduce myself
- [ ] ask information about a neighborhood
- [ ] ask permission to do something
- [ ] offer to help someone
- [ ] ask a favor of someone
- [ ] tell about things I did
- [ ] give advice to someone
- [ ] call about a housing problem

20

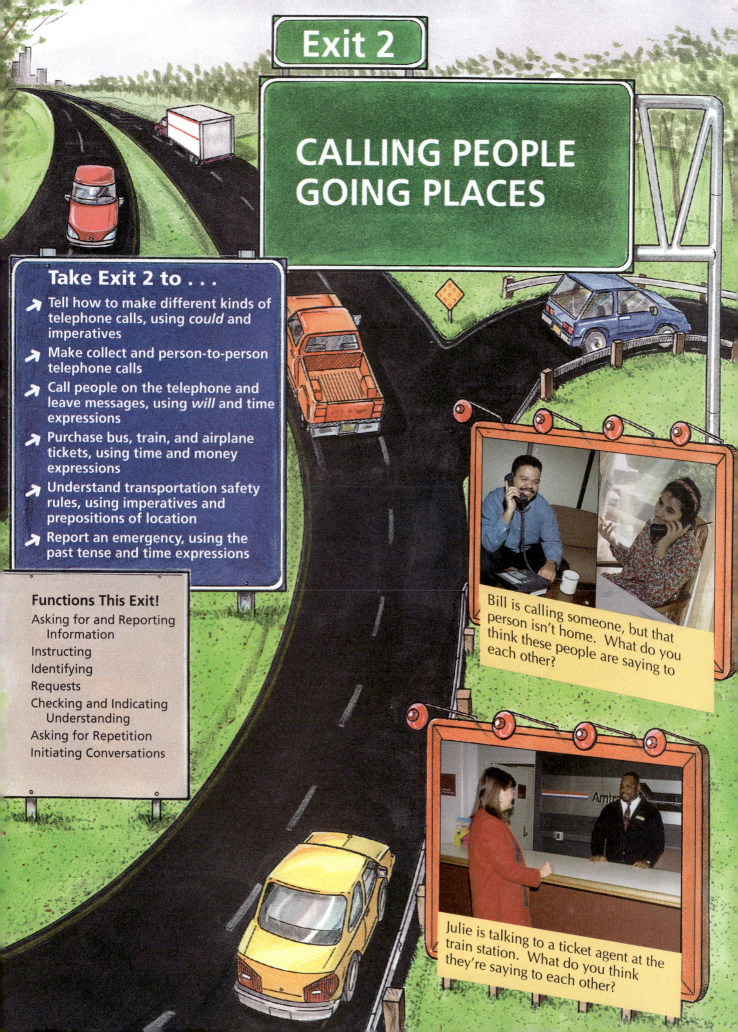

Exit 2

CALLING PEOPLE GOING PLACES

Take Exit 2 to . . .

↗ Tell how to make different kinds of telephone calls, using *could* and imperatives

↗ Make collect and person-to-person telephone calls

↗ Call people on the telephone and leave messages, using *will* and time expressions

↗ Purchase bus, train, and airplane tickets, using time and money expressions

↗ Understand transportation safety rules, using imperatives and prepositions of location

↗ Report an emergency, using the past tense and time expressions

Functions This Exit!

Asking for and Reporting Information
Instructing
Identifying
Requests
Checking and Indicating Understanding
Asking for Repetition
Initiating Conversations

Bill is calling someone, but that person isn't home. What do you think these people are saying to each other?

Julie is talking to a ticket agent at the train station. What do you think they're saying to each other?

make a long-distance call

A. Excuse me. Could you please tell me how to make a long-distance call?

B. Sure. Dial "one." Dial the area code. Then, dial the local phone number. Have you got it?

A. I think so. Let me see. I dial "one." I dial the area code. And then I . . . hmm. Could you repeat the last step?

B. Yes. Dial the local phone number.

A. Okay. I understand. Thanks very much.

A. Excuse me. Could you please tell me how to _____?

B. Sure. _____.

_____.

Then, _____.

Have you got it?

A. I think so. Let me see. I _____.

I _____.

And then I . . . hmm. Could you repeat the last step?

B. Yes. _____.

A. Okay. I understand. Thanks very much.

- *Pick up the receiver.*
- *Put the money in the coin slot.*
- *Dial the number.*

1 use this pay phone

- *Dial "zero."*
- *Dial the area code and local phone number.*
- *Tell the operator it's a collect call and give your name.*

2 make a collect call

- *Dial "zero."*
- *Dial the area code and local phone number.*
- *Tell the operator it's a person-to-person call and give the name of the person you're calling.*

3 make a person-to-person call

Ask someone how to do something. When the person tells you three things to do, don't forget to double-check to make sure you understand.

Fill It In!

Fill in the correct answer.

1. _____ the operator it's a collect call.
   - a. Tell *(circled)*
   - b. Dial

2. _____ the money in the coin slot.
   - a. Set
   - b. Put

3. _____ your name to the operator.
   - a. Give
   - b. Ask

4. _____ the local phone number.
   - a. Dial
   - b. Press

5. _____ the receiver.
   - a. Pull
   - b. Pick up

6. _____ the receiver.
   - a. Put down
   - b. Turn on

7. _____ a collect call.
   - a. Dial
   - b. Make

8. _____ the last step.
   - a. Repeat
   - b. Place

9. _____ "zero."
   - a. Get
   - b. Dial

10. _____ a pay phone.
    - a. Use
    - b. Get

11. Tell the _____ it's a collect call.
    - a. area code
    - b. operator

12. Dial _____ and then the area code.
    - a. "one"
    - b. the phone

Telephone Talk!

local phone number	operator	collect call	dial
person-to-person call	area code	long-distance call	put in

1. Tell the __operator__ you want to make a collect call.

2. You don't pay for the phone call when you make a _____.

3. Give the name of the person you're calling when you make a _____.

4. I had to _____ $2.00 when I called Philadelphia.

5. _____ the area code first, and then the local number.

6. You don't have to dial the area code. It's a _____.

7. When you make a long-distance call, you have to dial the _____. Then you dial the local phone number.

8. You have to dial "one," then the area code, then the local phone number to make a _____.

24

CrossTalk

Talk with a partner about making telephone calls.

Do you make collect calls?
Who do you call collect?
Why do you call those people collect?

Do you make person-to-person calls?
Who do you call person-to-person?
Why do you call person-to-person?

Report to the class about your "telephone" discussion.

More CrossTalk

Talk with a partner about making international telephone calls.

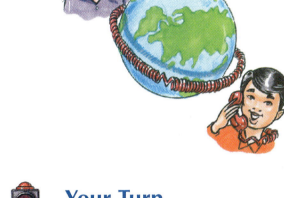

Do you ever make international calls?
To what countries?
Who do you call?
How much does it cost?

How do you make international calls?
Is it difficult?
What country codes do you know?

Report to the class about your discussion and make a master list on the board of the different countries around the world that students call.

Your Turn

For Writing and Discussion

Tell about the telephone service in your country. How do you make local calls, collect calls, person-to-person calls, and international calls? Is telephone service in your country efficient? Is it easy or difficult to make calls?

Community Connections

Bring to class a copy of your local telephone directory. Think of different tasks to ask a partner to do, using the directory. For example:

What's the area code of _____?
What's the country code for _____?
What's the telephone number of _____?

If your telephone book has "yellow pages" that list businesses, ask your partner to find out names and telephone numbers of different kinds of businesses that are listed.

A. Operator.

B. I want to make this a collect call, please.

A. What's your name?

B. Edward Bratt.

A. Did you say Edward Pratt?

B. No. Edward Bratt.

A. All right. One moment, please.

1 make this a person-to-person call

2 make this a collect call

3 make this a person-to-person call

4 make this a person-to-person collect call to Rose Wilson

5 charge this to my home phone

Make a collect or a person-to-person call to someone.

Matching Lines

Match and pronounce.

b	**1**	Do you have the ____?	a. dime		
	2	Do you have a ____?	b. time		
	3	His watch is ____.	a. cold		
	4	The weather is ____.	b. gold		
	5	Let's go with ____.	a. Sue		
	6	We went to the ____.	b. zoo		
	7	Let's play ____.	a. tennis		
	8	Hello. This is ____.	b. Dennis		
	9	We're at the ____.	a. peach		
	10	I'd like to eat a ____.	b. beach		

11	Are the pants too ____?	a. wrong
12	What did I do ____?	b. long
13	That was really ____.	a. fun
14	This is my ____.	b. son
15	Try on this ____.	a. code
16	Dial the area ____.	b. coat
17	Take the next ____.	a. train
18	I fixed the ____.	b. drain
19	What did you ____?	a. ear
20	This is my ____.	b. hear

Listen

Listen and choose the word you hear.

1 a. Helen
      b. Ellen

2 a. Nickie
      b. Mickie

3 a. Dannon
      b. Tannon

4 a. Bratt
      b. Pratt

5 a. nine
      b. five

6 a. seven
      b. eleven

7 a. Sales
      b. Zales

8 a. Deckler
      b. Teckler

9 a. door
      b. store

10 a. wife
      b. life

REFLECTIONS
When do people need to use the operator to make a telephone call? How much more expensive are operator-assisted calls?

Discuss in pairs or small groups, and then share your ideas with the class.

Community Connections

Think of five "telephone tasks" for a partner to do. For example:

Call (*name of store*). Ask if they sell (*name of article*).
Call (*name of theater*). Find out what time (*name of movie*) begins.
Call the bus station. Ask how often buses go to (*name of place*).
Call the train station. Ask if there is a train to (*name of place*).
Call the museum. Find out when the museum opens and closes.

Compare the results of everybody's phone calls.

A. May I please speak to Betty?
B. I'm afraid she isn't here right now.
A. Oh, I see. When will she be back?
B. She'll be back in an hour.
A. Okay. Thanks. I'll call back then.

A. May I please speak to Mrs. Arnold?

B. I'm sorry. She isn't here right now.

A. I see. Will she be back soon?

B. She won't be back until three. May I ask who's calling?

A. This is Bob Maxwell.

B. Do you want to leave a message?

A. Yes. Please ask her to call me when she gets back.

B. All right. I'll give her the message.

A. Thank you.

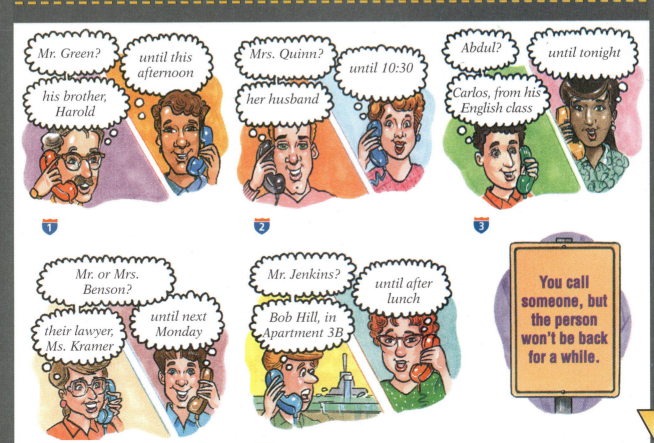

Constructions Ahead!

(I will)	I'll	
(He will)	He'll	
(She will)	She'll	
(It will)	It'll	be back soon.
(We will)	We'll	
(You will)	You'll	
(They will)	They'll	

1. Will Sally be back soon?   Yes, _she will_. _She'll_ be back in a few minutes.

2. Will you please call back?   Yes, _____. _____ call back in an hour.

3. Will Timmy finish his homework soon?   Yes, _____. _____ finish it in a little while.

4. Will your assistants be in the office today?   Yes, _____. _____ be in all afternoon.

5. Will you and your wife be home tonight?   Yes, _____. _____ be home all evening.

6. Will it be cloudy tomorrow?   Yes, _____. _____ be cloudy all day.

7. Will I see you at the party this Saturday?   Yes, _____. _____ see me with my new girlfriend.

More Constructions Ahead!

I	
He	
She	
It	won't be here until 3:00.
We	(will not)
You	
They	

1. Will you be back soon?   No, _I won't_. _I won't_ be back until after 5:00.

2. Will Mr. Wells call me today?   No, _____. _____ call you until tomorrow.

3. Will your sister be back soon?   No, _____. _____ be back until late tonight.

4. Will Mr. and Mrs. Lane be home tonight?   No, _____. _____ be home until after midnight.

5. Will the train be on time?   No, _____. _____ arrive until after 9:30.

6. Will you and your husband be home today?   No, _____. _____ be home until tonight.

7. Will I get a raise this year?   No, _____. _____ get a raise until next year.

Missing Lines

Fill in the missing lines in the conversation below and then practice the conversation with a partner. Compare different students' versions of the conversation.

A. Ms. Tyler's office.

B. ....

A. I'm afraid Ms. Tyler isn't here right now.

B. ....

A. No, I'm afraid she won't. She won't be here all day.

B. ....

A. I'm sorry. Mr. Kiley isn't in the office either.

B. ....

A. Yes, he will. He'll be in after 2:45. Do you want to leave a message?

B. Yes. Please tell Mr. Kiley ....
....

A. I'll give him the message.

Listen

Listen to the conversations and put the number under the correct memo.

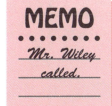

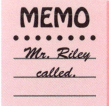

MEMO	MEMO	MEMO	MEMO	MEMO
Mr. Wiley called.	Call your wife.	Mr. Riley called.	Call Ms. White.	Mrs. Tyler called.
____	____	1	____	____

Community Connections

This is the Centerville Museum. Hours are from 9 A.M. to 5 P.M.

These days it is common for places such as movie theaters, museums, and airlines to have recorded messages for callers. Is this common where you live? What's your opinion of these recorded messages?

Just for fun, call a place that has a recorded message, write it down, and then compare what you heard with the messages that other students heard.

31

A. When is the next bus to Buffalo?

B. It's at 4:10.*

A. At 4:10?

B. Yes.

A. I'd like a round-trip ticket, please.

B. All right. That'll be twenty-four dollars and fifty cents ($24.50).

* 4:10 = four ten
2:37 = two thirty-seven
10:55 = ten fifty-five
6:25 = six twenty-five

† 3:07 = three "oh" seven
11:05 = eleven "oh" five

Match the Times

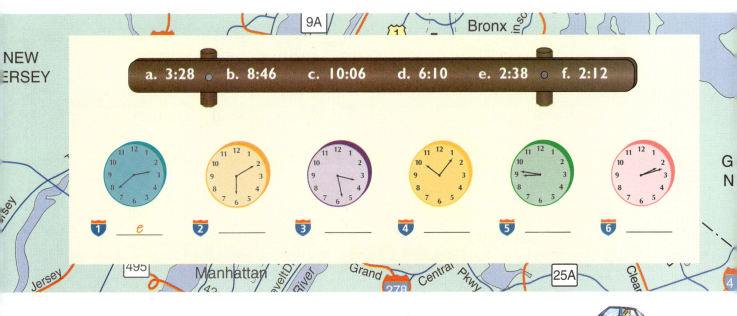

a. 3:28   b. 8:46   c. 10:06   d. 6:10   e. 2:38   f. 2:12

1. ___e___   2. _____   3. _____   4. _____   5. _____   6. _____

Listen

Listen and choose the correct answer.

1. a. It's at 4:50.
   b. It's $4.50.

2. a. It's at 10:10.
   b. It's $10.10.

3. a. It's at 11:00.
   b. It's $11.00.

4. a. It's at 8:20.
   b. It's $8.20.

5. a. It's at 9:10.
   b. It's $9.10.

6. a. It's at 2:15.
   b. It's $2.15.

7. a. It's at 12:00.
   b. It's $12.00.

8. a. It's at 5:35.
   b. It's $5.35.

What's the Time?

A.M. = in the morning   P.M. = in the afternoon, evening

12:00 A.M. = midnight   12:00 P.M. = noon
1:00 A.M. = 1:00 in the morning   1:00 P.M. = 1:00 in the afternoon
10:00 A.M. = 10:00 in the morning   10:00 P.M. = 10:00 in the evening

1. Lunch will be at 12:00 __P.M.__

2. The late movie starts at 10:30 ___.

3. Let's meet for dinner at 6:00 ___.

4. Breakfast is served beginning at 5:00 ___.

5. Our children go to bed at 9:00 ___.

6. The sun goes down at around 8:30 ___.

7. The sun usually comes up at about 6:15 ___.

8. That loud noise woke* us up at 3:15 ___.

9. We finally had lunch at 1:45 ___.

10. Our store is open sixteen hours a day. We open at 7:00 ___ and close at 11:00 ___.

*wake–woke

DESTINATION	ONE-WAY FARE	ROUND-TRIP TICKET	LEAVES
San Diego	$27.00	$50.00	10:50 A.M
San Francisco	$45.60	$87.40	11:00 A.M.
San Jose	$30.00	$58.00	3:45 P.M.
Santa Barbara	$28.00	$50.60	5:36 P.M.

1

When does the next bus leave for Santa Barbara?

It leaves at <u>5:36 P.M.</u> Do you want a round-trip or a one-way ticket?

One-way, please.

All right. That'll be _____.

2

How much is a round-trip ticket to San Diego?

It's _____. How many tickets do you want?

Two, please.

Okay. That'll be _____.

3

What time does the next bus leave for San Francisco?

At _____.

All right. I'd like one round-trip ticket, please.

That'll be _____.

4

I'd like a one-way ticket to San Jose.

All right. That'll be _____.

And what time does it leave?

It leaves at _____.

CrossTalk

Talk with a partner about traveling.

How do you usually travel
   long-distance?
Do you take the train? the plane?
   the bus?
Which of these do you prefer? Why?
Where do you usually go?

Report to the class about your
travel preferences.

Transportation Survey

Now interview ten people outside of class. Ask how they prefer to travel. Compare your findings with other students' and make a chart on the board of the results of your transportation survey.

InterActions

Get a copy of a train, plane, or long-distance bus schedule. You're now a "ticket agent" for that train, plane, or bus line. Other students in the class will ask you questions. For example:

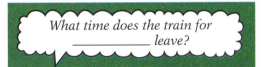

What time does the train for _____ leave?

What time does flight _____ arrive in _____?

How much does a one-way ticket to _____ cost?

Answer their questions about the schedule.

Your Turn

For Writing and Discussion

Tell about a bus, train, or plane trip you took.

Where did you go?
How did you get there?
Tell about the time you spent on the
   bus, train, or plane.

A. Excuse me. Please fasten your seat belt!
B. I'm sorry. I didn't hear you. What did you say?
A. I said, "Please fasten your seat belt!"
B. Oh, okay.

ExpressWays

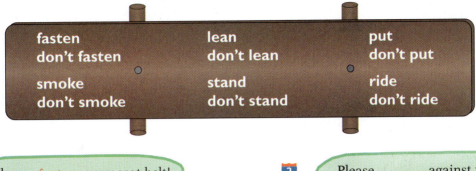

fasten	lean	put
don't fasten	don't lean	don't put
smoke	stand	ride
don't smoke	don't stand	don't ride

1 Please <u>fasten</u> your seat belt!

2 Please _____ against that door! You'll stop the train!

3 Please _____ behind the white line!

4 Please _____ outside!

5 Please _____ that bag under your seat!

6 Please _____ on that chair! You'll fall!

7 Please _____ your bicycles carefully!

8 Please _____ those dishes away yet!

Fill It In!

Fill in the correct preposition.

1 Did you put your purse _____ the seat?
    a. between
    (b.) under

2 Don't stand in front of him. Stand _____ him.
    a. under
    b. behind

3 Don't lean _____ the door.
    a. behind
    b. against

4 The waiter put flowers _____ all the tables.
    a. against
    b. on

5 I'm standing _____ Karen and Bob.
    a. on
    b. between

6 Please sit _____ me.
    a. between
    b. in front of

7 Put the cake _____ the two children.
    a. between
    b. against

8 I'm sorry. You can't smoke _____ this flight.
    a. with
    b. on

CrossTalk

Talk with a partner about transportation rules and regulations in your country. Then report to the class and compare how strict these rules are in different places.

INTERCHANGE

I Want to Report an Emergency!

A car just hit a pedestrian.

Diane Lockwood

on Washington Street, between *Second and Third Avenue*

A. Police.

B. I want to report an emergency!

A. Yes. Go ahead.

B. A car just hit* a pedestrian.

A. Where?

B. On Washington Street, between Second and Third Avenue.

A. Did you say Second and Third Avenue?

B. Yes. That's right.

A. What's your name?

B. Diane Lockwood.

A. All right. We'll be there right away.

* hit–hit

38

A. Police.

B. I want to report an emergency!

A. Yes. Go ahead.

B. _____.

A. Where?

B. _____.

A. Did you say _____?

B. Yes. That's right.

A. What's your name?

B. _____.

A. All right. We'll be there right away.

Somebody just robbed a grocery store.

Ken Johnson

1 at the corner of *Broadway and K Street*

There's a bad accident on Main Street.

Susan Bishop

2 in front of *the Hilton Hotel*

A man just had a heart attack.

Alberto Rodriguez

3 in the parking lot on *Maple Street*

Somebody just mugged a jogger in the park.

Clara Hopkins

4 near *the statue of Robert E. Lee*

You're reporting an emergency. Create an original conversation, using the model dialog above as a guide. Feel free to adapt and expand the model any way you wish.

Franco is a waiter in New York City. He has one week off every August for summer vacation. Last summer he decided to take a trip to California. He didn't want to go by plane. He really wanted to see the United States, so he decided to take the train from New York to California.

The train left* Penn Station in New York City on Monday at 10:30 P.M. Franco tried to sleep that night, but he couldn't because he was too excited. He knew this trip was a fantastic idea!

During the long trip, he looked out the window and watched the country go by. He saw large cities, small towns, and of course the beautiful countryside. He saw farms in Kansas, magnificent snow-capped mountains in Colorado, and the Mojave Desert between Arizona and California.

For five days, Franco didn't get off the train. He often took walks through the train and talked with the other passengers. Sometimes he rode* between the cars to get some fresh air. He had all his meals in the dining car.

Finally, at 2:45 P.M. on Friday, the train stopped in San Francisco. Franco was happy to get off the train! He called some of his friends, and they got together and ate* at an Italian restaurant in North Beach. On Saturday, he went to a museum in Golden Gate Park and had lunch at a restaurant near Ghirardelli Square.

On Sunday, Franco took a 9:20 A.M. flight back to New York. He looked out the window of the airplane and imagined the desert, mountains, farms, and cities below him. After a while, he closed his eyes and started to make plans for his next summer vacation!

True or False?

1. Franco works in a restaurant.
2. He has one month off every August.
3. He didn't go to California by plane because he wanted to see the countryside.
4. The train to California left in the morning.
5. The trip to California took a week.
6. Franco got off the train to get some fresh air.
7. The train arrived in the afternoon.
8. Franco was with his friends on Friday.
9. Franco stayed in California for a week.
10. He went back to New York by train.

40

*leave–left
ride–rode
eat–ate

Matching Lines

_c_ **1** The train left at ____.   a. dining car

____ **2** We ate in the ____.   b. train station

____ **3** We got our ticket at the ____.   c. 9:15 A.M.

____ **4** There was an accident on ____.   d. a new restaurant

____ **5** We had a picnic in ____.   e. Summer Avenue

____ **6** I had dinner at ____.   f. the park

____ **7** Don't lean against ____.   g. my two best friends

____ **8** I sat between ____.   h. the shopping mall

____ **9** Our new house is near ____.   i. the door

____ **10** Don't park here from ____.   j. midnight

____ **11** We left the party at ____.   k. the bank

____ **12** The bus stopped in front of ____.   l. 9:00 to 4:00

Listen

Listen and choose the word to complete each sentence.

1 (a.) those cars
 b. my car

2 a. the street
 b. your house

3 a. the afternoon
 b. a busy street

4 a. Second Street
 b. an apartment

5 a. us
 b. the park

6 a. a bus station
 b. an umbrella

7 a. 3:30 A.M.
 b. the afternoon

8 a. the table
 b. the basement

9 a. the white line
 b. my car

Your Turn

For Writing and Discussion

Franco really enjoyed his vacation. Tell about a vacation YOU took. Where did you go? How did you get there? What did you do on your vacation?

REFLECTIONS
Compare long-distance travel in different countries you know. What's it like to travel by bus? by train? by airplane?

Discuss in pairs or small groups, and then share your ideas with the class.

Looking Back

☐ **Telephone**
area code
coin slot
collect call
home phone
local phone number
long-distance call
message
number
operator
pay phone
person-to-person call
receiver

charge
dial

☐ **Transportation**
boat
bus
flight
train

ticket
one-way ticket
round-trip ticket

cars
door
seat
seat belt
white line

fasten
lean
ride
smoke
stand

☐ **Emergencies**
accident
emergency
heart attack
pedestrian

hit
mug
report
rob

Now Leaving Exit 2 Construction Area

☐ **Imperatives**
☐ **Future: Will**
☐ **Prepositions of Location**
☐ **Time Expressions**

Sorry for the inconvenience. For more information see page 170.

ExpressWays Checklist
I can . . .

☐ tell how to make different kinds of telephone calls
☐ make collect and person-to-person telephone calls
☐ call people on the telephone and leave messages
☐ purchase bus, train, and airplane tickets
☐ understand transportation safety rules
☐ report an emergency

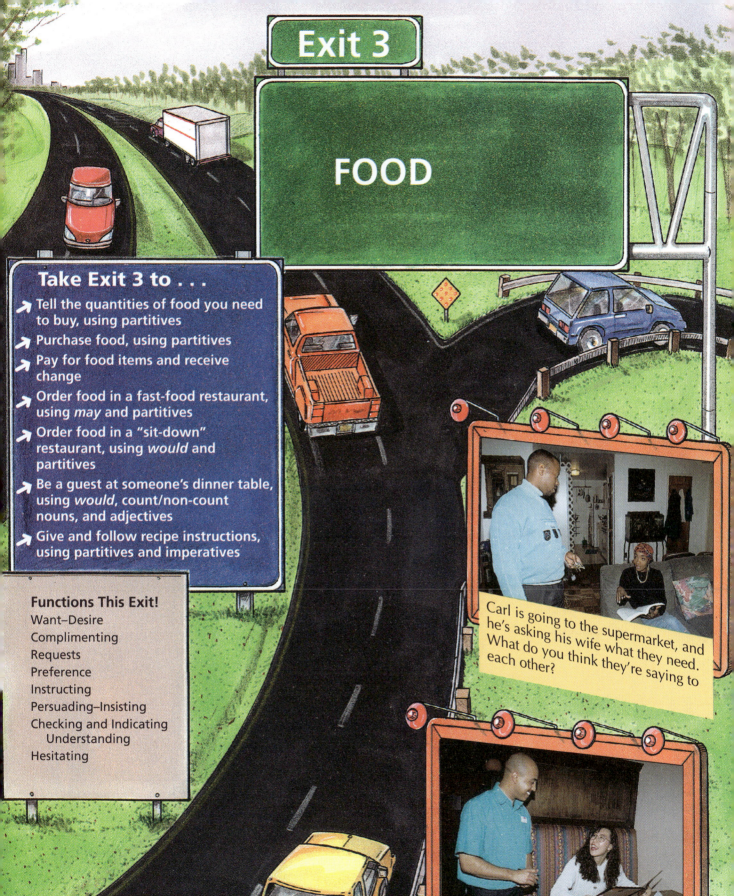

Exit 3

FOOD

Take Exit 3 to . . .

➔ Tell the quantities of food you need to buy, using partitives

➔ Purchase food, using partitives

➔ Pay for food items and receive change

➔ Order food in a fast-food restaurant, using *may* and partitives

➔ Order food in a "sit-down" restaurant, using *would* and partitives

➔ Be a guest at someone's dinner table, using *would*, count/non-count nouns, and adjectives

➔ Give and follow recipe instructions, using partitives and imperatives

Functions This Exit!

Want–Desire
Complimenting
Requests
Preference
Instructing
Persuading–Insisting
Checking and Indicating
   Understanding
Hesitating

Carl is going to the supermarket, and he's asking his wife what they need. What do you think they're saying to each other?

Donna is ordering food at a restaurant. What do you think she and the waiter are saying to each other?

A. Do we need anything from the supermarket?

B. Yes. We need a quart of milk.

A. A quart?

B. Yes.

A. Anything else?

B. No, I don't think so.

A. Okay. I'll get a quart of milk.

B. Thanks.

a quart of milk

a pound of apples

a gallon of orange juice

2 boxes of rice

a dozen eggs

2 jars of mayonnaise

You need a quart, pound, gallon, box, dozen, or jar of something at the supermarket.

What Do You Want Me to Get?

A. Could you do me a favor?

B. Sure. What is it?

A. We need a few things from the supermarket.

B. What do you want me to get?

A. A can of tuna fish, a loaf of white bread, and a head of lettuce.

B. A can of tuna fish, a loaf of white bread, and a head of lettuce. Anything else?

A. No. That's all. Thanks.

a can of tuna fish

a loaf of white bread

a head of lettuce

1.
a dozen oranges — a pound of butter — a bunch of bananas

2.
a gallon of skim milk — a bottle of ketchup — a jar of mayonnaise

3.
a bag of potato chips — 2 loaves of whole wheat bread — half a gallon of apple juice

4.
a pint of vanilla ice cream — half a dozen eggs — 2 bunches of grapes

5.
a jar of peanut butter — a quart of chocolate milk — a box of chocolate chip cookies

Ask a family member to get a few things from the supermarket.

45

Fill It In!

Fill in the correct word.

1 I'd like a —— of cookies.
    a. dozen
    (b.) box

2 We need a —— eggs.
    a. pound
    b. dozen

3 I got a —— of mayonnaise.
    a. jar
    b. box

4 I'll get a —— of orange juice.
    a. quart
    b. box

5 How many —— of apples do we need?
    a. pounds
    b. jars

6 Buy a —— of milk, please.
    a. dozen
    b. gallon

7 We need a —— of lettuce.
    a. head
    b. bunch

8 Please get a —— of tuna fish.
    a. bag
    b. can

9 I'd like a —— of chocolate ice cream.
    a. pint
    b. bag

10 Buy a —— of bread at the supermarket.
    a. quart
    b. loaf

11 We need a —— of ketchup.
    a. box
    b. bottle

12 Please don't forget to buy a —— of bananas.
    a. bunch
    b. head

Listen

What food items do you hear?

1 (a.)  b.   (c.)

2 a. b. c.

3 a. b. c.

4 a. b. c.

5 a. b. c.

6 a. b. c.

7 a. b. c.

8 a. b. c.

9 a. b. c.

10 a. b. c.

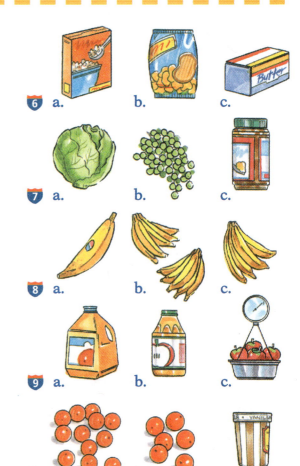

46

Matching Lines

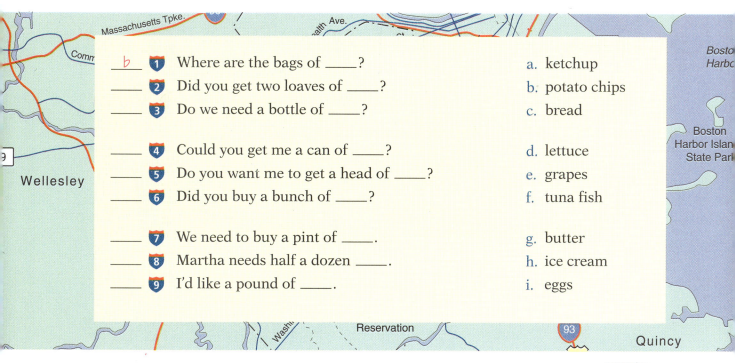

__b__ **1** Where are the bags of ____?

____ **2** Did you get two loaves of ____?

____ **3** Do we need a bottle of ____?

____ **4** Could you get me a can of ____?

____ **5** Do you want me to get a head of ____?

____ **6** Did you buy a bunch of ____?

____ **7** We need to buy a pint of ____.

____ **8** Martha needs half a dozen ____.

____ **9** I'd like a pound of ____.

a. ketchup

b. potato chips

c. bread

d. lettuce

e. grapes

f. tuna fish

g. butter

h. ice cream

i. eggs

Cultural Intersections

When people go food shopping, they might buy a **can** of tuna fish, a **jar** of mayonnaise, a **bottle** of ketchup, a **bag** of potato chips, a **box** of cereal, or perhaps a **pound** of steak.

My Shopping List

a can of . . . .

a jar of . . . .

a bottle of . . . .

a bag of . . . .

a box of . . . .

a pound/kilo of . . . .

How about you? What do you typically buy when YOU go shopping? Fill out the following list with foods you typically buy, and then compare your list with other students' lists.

CrossTalk

With a group of students in your class, make a shopping list for a class party.

What foods will you buy?
How much of each?

Compare your list with the lists made by other groups in the class.

For fun, ask your teacher if you can shop for the food on your lists and REALLY have a class party!

A. May I help you?

B. Yes, please. I want a pound of roast beef.

A. Anything else?

B. Yes. A dozen rolls.

A. All right. That's a pound of roast beef and a dozen rolls. Is that it?

B. Yes. That's it.

Order some food at the deli counter of a supermarket.

Timmy Isn't Feeling Well

Circle the correct word.

A. What's the matter, Timmy?

B. I have a stomachache.

A. I see. What did you eat today?

B. Some hot dogs.

A. Hmm. How many hot dogs did you eat?

B. Maybe half a ((dozen) bunch)[1].

A. Anything else?

B. I ate one big (piece   bag)[2] of potato chips, and I had a (piece   bottle)[3] of soda. Then I had dessert.

A. What did you have for dessert?

B. Some cookies.

A. Did you eat a lot of cookies?

B. Only one (jar   box)[4]. I ate them with chocolate ice cream.

A. How much ice cream did you have? A (jar   pint)[5]?

B. Well, I had a (loaf   pint)[6] of chocolate, and then I had a (pound   quart)[7] of vanilla.

Fill It In!

| gallon • dozen | jars | bottles | | boxes | bags | pieces • dozen |

I think we're all set for the picnic. I'm taking a ___dozen___[1] hot dogs, two _____[2] of ketchup, two _____[3] of mustard, and a _____[4] of apple juice. I'm also taking twenty _____[5] of chicken, four or five _____[6] of potato chips, about three _____[7] rolls, and two or three _____[8] of cookies. Do you think that's enough?

CrossTalk

Do you like to go on picnics? Talk with a partner about where you usually go on picnics and the kinds of foods you usually take with you.

REFLECTIONS
Compare food shopping in different countries you know. Are the stores large or small? How many different products do they have? Are there many different choices for each product?

Discuss in pairs or small groups, and then share your ideas with the class.

A. That'll be seven twenty-five ($7.25).

B. Seven twenty-five?

A. Yes.

B. Here's ten ($10).

A. All right. Your change is two dollars and seventy-five cents ($2.75). Here you are.

B. Thank you.

A. Have a nice day.

1. $1.15

2. $3.57

3. $8.40

4. $6.08

5. $.02

You're a cashier at a supermarket. Tell a customer how much money he or she owes, and give the person change.

ExpressWays

1.
That'll be $46.24.

Here's fifty.

All right. Your change is ___$3.76___.

2.
That comes to $13.56.

Here's twenty.

Okay. Your change is _____.

3.
With tax, that comes to $7.52.

Here's ten.

And your change is _____.

4.
That comes to $89.98.

Here's a hundred.

Okay. Your change is _____.

Listen

Listen and choose the correct number.

1 a. $30.15	**3** a. $17.06	**5** a. $28.00	**7** a. $5.00
(b.) $13.50	b. $72.36	b. $ .28	b. $9.00
2 a. $ .45	**4** a. $ .60	**6** a. $ 2.42	**8** a. $12.50
b. $4.05	b. $60.00	b. $10.42	b. $ 1.25

Community Connections

With a partner, make a shopping list for four people for seven days. Visit a local supermarket and write down the prices of the foods on your list. After your "shopping trip," compare your list and food prices with other students'.

Who spent the most money?
Who spent the least money?
Who bought too much food?
Who bought too little food?
Who bought the most nutritious food?
Who bought the most *junk* food?

A. Welcome to Burger Town. May I help you?

B. Yes. I'd like a hamburger and an order of french fries.

A. Do you want anything to drink with that?

B. Yes. I'll have a cup of coffee.

A. Okay. That's a hamburger, an order of french fries, and a cup of coffee. Is that for here or to go?

B. For here.

A. That comes to three dollars and thirteen cents ($3.13), please.

B. Here you are.

A. And here's your change. Your food will be ready in a moment.

a hamburger

an order of french fries

a cup of coffee

for here
$3.13

a cheeseburger *a small order of french fries* *a small orange soda*

1 to go
$2.65

a roast beef sandwich *a small salad* *a chocolate shake*

2 for here
$5.04

2 fish sandwiches *2 large orders of french fries* *a medium Coke*

3 to go
$7.83

2 tacos *an order of refried beans* *a large iced tea*

4 for here
$4.80

20 pieces of chicken *2 containers of cole slaw* *10 lemonades*

5 to go
$27.94

Order food at a fast-food restaurant.

Matching Lines

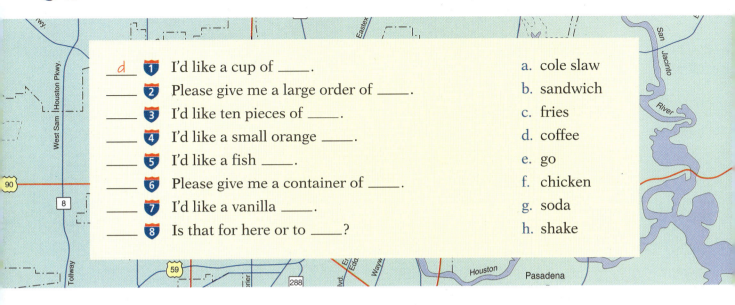

d   **1** I'd like a cup of _____.

_____ **2** Please give me a large order of _____.

_____ **3** I'd like ten pieces of _____.

_____ **4** I'd like a small orange _____.

_____ **5** I'd like a fish _____.

_____ **6** Please give me a container of _____.

_____ **7** I'd like a vanilla _____.

_____ **8** Is that for here or to _____?

a. cole slaw
b. sandwich
c. fries
d. coffee
e. go
f. chicken
g. soda
h. shake

CrossTalk

Talk with a partner about fast-food restaurants.

Are there fast-food restaurants in your city
or town?
What do they serve?
Do you ever go to fast-food restaurants?
Which ones?
What do you usually order?

As a class, discuss students' "fast-food" experiences.

Community Connections

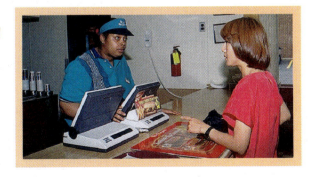

Visit a fast-food restaurant in your area. Make a list of the foods they serve and how much they cost. Order something and see how it tastes! Then compare with other students' findings and decide as a class which fast-food restaurant in your area is the best.

InterActions

Transform your classroom into a fast-food restaurant! Create a menu. Decide on the prices. Bring in props. Arrange the room into an ordering area and an eating area. Some students are workers. Others are customers. It's a very busy day today at your fast-food restaurant!

53

I'd Like the Chicken

rice or a baked potato?

A. What would you like?

B. I'd like the chicken.

A. All right. And would you prefer rice or a baked potato with that?

B. I'd prefer a baked potato.

A. And would you like anything to drink?

B. Yes. Let me see . . . I'll have a glass of milk.

A. Okay. That's the chicken with a baked potato, and a glass of milk.

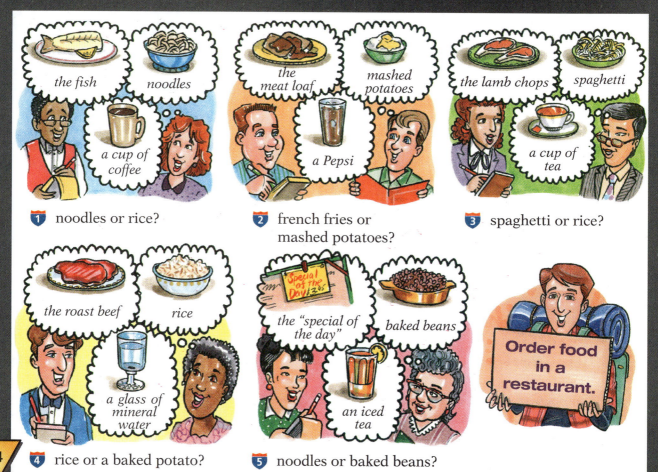

1. noodles or rice?

2. french fries or mashed potatoes?

3. spaghetti or rice?

4. rice or a baked potato?

5. noodles or baked beans?

Order food in a restaurant.

54

Listen

You will hear four conversations at a restaurant. Put the number next to the correct food items.

Appetizers

_____ egg rolls
_____ mushrooms

_____ bread and cheese
1 small salad

Main Dishes

_____ roast beef
_____ lamb chops
_____ fish

1 fried chicken
_____ spaghetti and meatballs
_____ tacos

Drinks

_____ iced tea
_____ mineral water

_____ orange soda
1 lemonade

InterActions

With a partner, complete the following conversation and then present your restaurant scenes to the class. Compare with other students' versions.

A. Is everything all right with your meal?

B. Well, actually this . . . . is cold!

A. I'm terrible sorry. I'll take it back to the kitchen.

B. Could you also take back this . . . . ? It isn't cooked enough.

A. I see. Anything else?

B. Yes. Could we please have two more glasses of . . . . ?

A. Of course. Can I get you anything else?

B. Yes. We'd like to order . . . .

A. Do you prefer . . . . or . . . . ?

B. . . . . , please.

CrossTalk

Talk with a partner about your favorite restaurant. Why is it your favorite? What do you recommend on the menu? When other students tell about their restaurants, make a "class guide" to favorite restaurants in your area.

meatballs

salad

A. Would you like a few more meatballs?

B. They're delicious . . . but no, thank you.

A. Oh, come on! Have a few more.

B. All right. But please . . . not too many.

A. Would you like a little more salad?

B. It's very good . . . but no, thank you.

A. Oh, come on! Have a little more.

B. All right. But please . . . not too much.

1 mushrooms

2 ice cream

3 cake

4 cookies

5 pie

You're a guest in someone's home. The person offers you more food, but remember . . . not too much, and not too many!

Constructions Ahead!

How much?	How many?
too much	too many
a little	a few

1 _____ orange juice do you want?
   (a.) How much
   b. How many

Not too _____.
   a. much
   b. many

2 Here! Have _____ more meatballs!
   a. a few
   b. a little

I already ate too _____.
   a. much
   b. many

3 I'd like _____ more cake, please.
   a. a few
   b. a little

All right. But not too _____.
   a. much
   b. many

4 May I have _____ more pie?
   a. a few
   b. a little

Okay. But not too _____.
   a. much
   b. many

5 _____ cookies do you want?
   a. How much
   b. How many

Just _____.
   a. a little
   b. a few

Listen

Listen and choose the correct food.

1 a.   (b.)
3 a.   b.
5 a.   b.

2 a.   b.
4 a.   b.
6 a.   b.

Cultural Intersections

Tell about meals in your country.

When do people usually have breakfast? What do they typically eat for breakfast?
When do people usually have lunch? What do they typically eat for lunch?
When do people usually have dinner? What do they typically eat for dinner?

INTERCHANGE

Can You Tell Me the Recipe?

A. Your cake was delicious. Can you tell me the recipe?

B. Sure. First, mix together a cup of flour, a teaspoon of salt, and two tablespoons of water.

A. I see.

B. Then, add half a cup of sugar. Are you with me so far?

A. Yes. I'm following you.

B. Okay. Next, add two eggs.

A. Uh-húh.

B. And then, put the mixture into a baking pan and bake for one hour at 350 degrees. Have you got all that?

A. Yes, I've got it. Thanks.

A. Your _____ was delicious. Can you tell me the recipe?

B. Sure. First, _____.

A. I see.

B. Then, _____.
Are you with me so far?

A. Yes. I'm following you.

B. Okay. Next, _____.

A. Uh-húh.

B. And then, _____.
Have you got all that?

A. Yes, I've got it. Thanks.

You're a dinner guest at somebody's home. Compliment the host or hostess and ask for a recipe, using the model dialog above as a guide. Feel free to adapt and expand the model any way you wish.

Crossed Lines

The instructions for the following recipes are all mixed up! Put the instructions in the correct order. Then complete the conversations and practice them with another student in your class.

____ **put the mixture into a baking pan**

__1__ **mix together sugar and butter**

____ **add one egg and a bag of chocolate chips**

____ **bake for 12 minutes**

> These cookies are delicious. Can you tell me the recipe?

> Sure. First, _____.
> Then, _____.
> Next, _____.
> And then, _____.

____ **add a cup of bread crumbs**

____ **bake for an hour**

____ **put the mixture into a loaf pan**

____ **mix together ground beef, onions, and mushrooms**

> Your meat loaf was very good. Could you tell me the recipe?

> Certainly. First, _____.
> Then, _____.
> Next, _____.
> And then, _____.

____ **add mushrooms and onions**

____ **mix the rice with carrots and raisins**

____ **cook a cup of rice for half an hour**

____ **put the mixture in the refrigerator for 2 hours**

> This rice salad is delicious! Is it easy?

> Yes, it is. First, _____.
> Then, _____.
> Next, _____.
> And then, _____.

59

_____ bake it for one and a half hours at 350 degrees

_____ put salt, pepper, and garlic all over the roast

_____ put it on a rack in the oven

_____ serve it with baked potatoes and a salad

This roast beef is excellent! Can you tell me the recipe?

Sure. First, _____.
Then, _____.
Next, _____.
And then, _____.

ExpressWays

Circle the correct word.

A. This fruit salad is delicious!

B. Well, it's easy to make. Cut three (sugar (bananas))[1], four (juice apples)[2], and a bunch of (lemonade grapes)[3] into small pieces. (Mix Add)[4] together, and then add half a cup of (orange juice orange)[5]. Put the (mixture recipe)[6] in the refrigerator for about an hour.

A. Thanks for the recipe. It's really a great fruit salad.

B. I'm glad you like (it them)[7]. Have a (few little)[8] more.

A. Okay. But not too (many much)[9]. I already had two (bowls pieces)[10].

Your Turn

For Writing and Discussion

What's your favorite recipe? Is it easy or difficult to make? Write the instructions and share your recipe with other students in your class.

If you wish, you can publish a **Class Recipe Book** of everybody's favorite recipes.

Reading: *Saving Time*

In the United States, many people try to save time. In many families, both the husband and wife work full-time, so their free time is very important to them. They look for quick and convenient ways to do their shopping and the other things they *need* to do, so that they will have free time for the things they *want* to do.

Many years ago, people had to go to the fish market to buy fish, to the butcher for meat and chicken, to the fruit market for fresh fruit, and to the bakery for bread and rolls. Nowadays, most people go to just one place. They can buy fruit, bread, meat, fresh vegetables, and frozen foods at their local supermarket. They can also buy things for the house, such as pots and pans, and brooms and buckets.

When Americans eat out, they often go to fast-food restaurants. Breakfast, lunch, and dinner are always ready. People order their meals at the counter and wait for their food for just a few seconds or minutes. Then they carry the food to a table, eat it, and throw their trash away. It takes only twenty minutes or so to eat a meal at a fast-food restaurant.

Supermarkets and fast-food restaurants are important to people in the United States. They are quick and convenient, and that's what people want when they are looking for ways to save time.

True or False?

1. Most Americans do their shopping at supermarkets.
2. Many years ago, people went to a butcher to buy lamb chops.
3. A bakery is a good place to buy bananas, grapes, lettuce, and other fruits and vegetables.
4. People don't have to shop at fish markets, butcher shops, fruit markets, and bakeries because they can buy all those things in just one place.
5. You can buy brooms, gloves, and soap at most American supermarkets.
6. It's convenient to eat at fast-food restaurants.
7. At fast-food restaurants, people usually have to wait for their food for twenty minutes.
8. At fast-food restaurants, waiters and waitresses bring food to the tables.
9. According to the reading, time is important because so many people work full-time.

Your Turn

For Writing and Discussion

How about you? Do you buy your food in special shops, or do you go to supermarkets? Do you eat in fast-food restaurants often? Do you think it's important to save time this way? Compare your ideas with the opinions of other students in your class.

Food Items

apple
banana
beans
  baked beans
  refried beans
beef
  ground beef
bread
  white bread
  whole wheat
    bread
butter
cake
cheese
  American
    cheese
  Swiss cheese
cheeseburger
chicken
coffee

cole slaw
cookies
  chocolate
    chip cookies
donut
egg
fish
flour
grapes
hamburger
hot dog
ice cream
  vanilla ice
    cream
juice
  apple juice
ketchup
lamb chop
lemonade
lettuce
mayonnaise

meatballs
meat loaf
milk
  chocolate
    milk
  skim milk
mineral water
mushrooms
mustard
noodles
orange
orange juice
peanut butter
pie
potato
  baked potato
  french fries
  mashed
    potatoes
  potato chips

potato salad
rice
roast beef
rolls
salad
salt
sandwich
  fish sandwich
  roast beef
    sandwich
shake
  chocolate
    shake
soda
  Coke
  orange soda
  Pepsi
spaghetti
sugar

taco
tea
  iced tea
tuna fish
water

Food Units

bag
bottle
box
bunch
can
dozen
gallon
head
jar
loaf–loaves
piece
pint
pound
quart

half a cup
half a dozen
half a gallon
half a pound
tablespoon
teaspoon

container
cup
glass

order
piece

small
medium
large

Purchasing Food

change
for here

"special of
  the day"
to go

Describing Food

delicious
excellent
fantastic
very good

Recipes

add
bake
baking pan
350 degrees
mix together
mixture
recipe

Now Leaving Exit 3 Construction Area

- ☐ **Partitives**
- ☐ **Count/Non-Count Nouns**
- ☐ **Imperatives**
- ☐ **May**
- ☐ **Would**

Sorry for the inconvenience. For more information see page 171.

ExpressWays Checklist

I can . . .

- ☐ tell the quantities of food I need to buy
- ☐ purchase food
- ☐ pay for food items and receive change
- ☐ order food in a fast-food restaurant
- ☐ order food in a "sit-down" restaurant
- ☐ be a guest at someone's dinner table
- ☐ give and follow recipe instructions

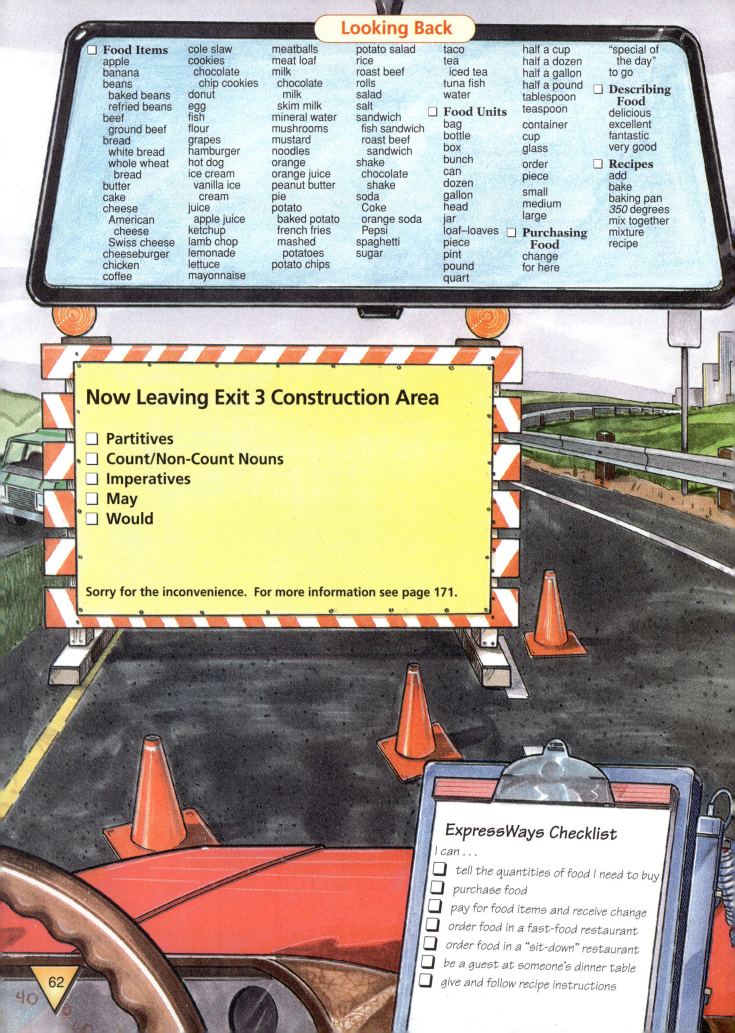

REST STOP
Take a break!
Have a conversation!

Here are some scenes from Exits 1, 2, and 3.

Who do you think these people are?
What do you think they're talking about?

In pairs or small groups, create conversations based on these scenes and act them out.

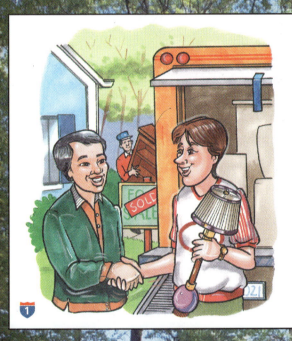

Exit 4

PERSONAL FINANCES

Take Exit 4 to . . .

- Evaluate the affordability of items in a store, using comparatives
- Evaluate the affordability of items in a store, using superlatives
- Budget your money, using *should, have to,* and *going to*
- Accomplish everyday banking procedures, using imperatives
- Discuss balancing a checkbook
- Understand denominations of money, using *should* and the past tense
- Evaluate payment of household bills, using ordinal numbers
- Deal effectively with errors on household bills

Functions This Exit!

Remembering/Forgetting
Describing
Agreement/Disagreement
Certainty/Uncertainty
Obligation
Intention
Advice–Suggestions
Asking for and Reporting
   Information

Ana and Ruben are shopping in a store, and they're concerned because everything is so expensive. What do you think they're saying to each other?

Daniel and Tess are paying their household bills. What do you think they're saying to each other?

I Don't Think We Can Afford It

refrigerator
large

sofa
comfortable

A. Which refrigerator do you like?

B. I like this one. It's very large.

A. I know. It's larger than that one, but it's also more expensive.

B. Hmm. You're right.

A. I don't think we can afford it.

B. I suppose not.

A. Which sofa do you like?

B. I like this one. It's very comfortable.

A. I know. It's more comfortable than that one, but it's also more expensive.

B. Hmm. You're right.

A. I don't think we can afford it.

B. I suppose not.

1 air conditioner
quiet

2 rug
attractive

3 crib
nice

4 stereo system
good*

5 computer
powerful

You like something in a store, but you can't afford it. It's too expensive.

*good–better

66

Constructions Ahead!

quiet – quieter	comfortable – more comfortable	
large – larger	attractive – more attractive	
big – bigger	powerful – more powerful	good – better
pretty – prettier	expensive – more expensive	

1. This fan isn't very quiet.
Look at this one. It's much _quieter_.

2. This washing machine isn't very big.
How about this one? It's much _____.

3. This chair isn't very attractive.
Look at THIS one. It's _____ than that one.

4. These blankets are very nice.
You're right. But THESE blankets are _____ than those.

5. This car isn't very powerful.
Try THIS car. It's _____ than that one.

6. These gloves aren't comfortable.
Try these. They're _____ than those.

7. This is a good CD player.
I think this one is _____.

8. This doll is very pretty.
You're right. But I think this one is even _____!

ExpressWays

1.
I'd love to buy a color TV, but they're expensive.

I know. A black-and-white TV is _cheaper_ .

2.
This fan is driving me crazy! It's so noisy!

I know. A new one will be much _____.

3.
I'm gaining weight. My bathrobe is too small.

Hmm. I think you need to buy a _____ one.

4.
The weather is really hot!

Don't worry. It'll be _____ tomorrow.

5.
This old sofa is really uncomfortable!

You're right. We need to buy a _____ one!

6.
Please don't wear that tie! It's ugly! Try to find a _____ one!

Listen

Listen and decide what these people are talking about.

1. (a.) computer
b. rug

2. a. CD player
b. coat

3. a. blouse
b. boots

4. a. weather
b. air conditioner

5. a. chair
b. stereo system

6. a. counter
b. sweater

7. a. dining room
b. dining room table

8. a. crib
b. parrot

9. a. department store
b. salespeople

Fill It In!

Fill in the correct comparative.

John and Barbara Wilson are looking for a new apartment. Yesterday they saw a nice apartment on Peach Street. Right now they're looking at an apartment on Oak Avenue.

JOHN: This street is very nice, but I think Peach Street is *(quiet)* _____quieter_____[1].

BARBARA: You're right. It's very noisy here, but this building is *(attractive)* _____[2] than the building on Peach Street.

JOHN: You're right. This is a *(pretty)* _____[3] building, but I think the apartment on Peach Street will be *(comfortable)* _____[4] than this one. The living room there is much *(large)* _____[5], and the bathroom is *(nice)* _____[6].

BARBARA: Hmm. But this kitchen is *(modern)*_____[7] than the one on Peach Street. Look at this dishwasher! I think this apartment is much *(good)* _____[8] than the other one.

JOHN: Okay. It's *(attractive)* _____[9], it's *(modern)* _____[10], but it's also *(expensive)* _____[11]. I don't think we can afford it.

BARBARA: I suppose not.

Community Connections

Visit a store in your area and do some comparison shopping! Decide on a product you would like to "buy" — perhaps a TV set, a stereo system, or even a computer. Compare the prices and features of different brands. Ask salespeople for their recommendations.

> *The picture on the Zuny TV is brighter and clearer than the picture on the Apex.*

> *I recommend the ABC Computer. It's cheaper and more powerful than the XYZ Computer.*

You might even want to compare the price of the same product at two different stores.

> *I went to Wally's and to TV Town. Guess what! The Zuny is $50 cheaper at Wally's.*

Report your findings to the class and see what other students learned on their comparison shopping trips.

Can You Show Me a Less Expensive One?

a firm mattress
$300

a comfortable armchair
$450

A. May I help you?

B. Yes. I'm looking for a firm mattress.

A. Take a look at this one. It's the firmest mattress in the store.

B. How much is it?

A. Three hundred dollars ($300).

B. I see. Can you show me a less expensive one?

A. Certainly. I'll be happy to.

A. May I help you?

B. Yes. I'm looking for a comfortable armchair.

A. Take a look at this one. It's the most comfortable armchair in the store.

B. How much is it?

A. Four hundred and fifty dollars ($450).

B. I see. Can you show me a less expensive one?

A. Certainly. I'll be happy to.

1. a large kitchen table
$225

2. a lightweight typewriter
$185

3. a big bookcase
$540

4. a good* cassette player
$160

5. a powerful computer
$3,750

Ask a salesperson in a store to show you a less expensive item. The one you like is too expensive.

*good–the best

Constructions Ahead!

firm – the firmest	lightweight – the most lightweight
large – the largest	powerful – the most powerful
big – the biggest	good – the best

REFLECTIONS
Compare shopping in different countries you know. Do items have *fixed* prices, or can you *bargain* with the salesperson to make the price lower?

Discuss in pairs or small groups, and then share your ideas with the class.

1. I'm looking for a powerful cassette player. — This is ___the most powerful___ one we have.

2. Can you show me a very firm sofa? — Certainly. This is _____ sofa in the store.

3. I'm looking for a good stereo system. — This is _____ one we have.

4. I'm looking for a dependable dryer. — Take a look at this one. It's _____ dryer they make.

5. We're looking for some very big bookcases. — These are _____ bookcases in the store.

6. My son needs a lightweight jacket. — How about this one? It's _____ jacket we have.

7. I'm looking for a tall lamp. — How about this one? It's _____ lamp in the store.

8. I'd like a very talkative parrot. — You'll like this one. It's _____ parrot we have.

Matching Lines

__d__ ① This bicycle is too heavy!

_____ ② This belt is too large!

_____ ③ This jacket is too tight!

_____ ④ This sofa is very ugly!

_____ ⑤ This ticket costs $25!

_____ ⑥ This tennis racket is too light!

_____ ⑦ What a soft mattress!

a. It's the smallest one in the store.

b. It's the most attractive one in the store.

c. It's the firmest one we have.

d. It's the most lightweight one we have.

e. It's the heaviest one we have.

f. It's the loosest one we carry.

g. It's the cheapest one we have.

Fill It In!

Fill in the correct form of the adjective.

Susan went to the Davis Furniture Company last weekend because there was a big storewide sale. She needed a sofa for her living room. A sales clerk in the Furniture Department tried* to help her. First he showed her _(attractive)_ ___the most attractive___¹ sofa in the store. It was made of leather, and it was very _(nice)_ _____², but it was also _(expensive)_ _____³ sofa in the store! Susan was sorry it wasn't on sale.

The sales clerk then showed her a white sofa. It was _(comfortable)_ _____⁴ one in the store. Susan tried it out. It certainly was _(comfortable)_ _____⁵ than the leather sofa. It was also _(cheap)_ _____⁶ than the leather one, but it was still too _(expensive)_ _____⁷. It wasn't on sale, either.

Finally, she saw a light blue sofa in the back of the store. It was very _(comfortable)_ _____⁸, and it wasn't very _(expensive)_ _____⁹. Susan thought it was _(nice)_ _____¹⁰ sofa in the store! And it was on sale! It was 40 percent off! It was _(cheap)_ _____¹¹ sofa in the store. Susan was thrilled. She bought* _(good)_ _____¹² sofa in the store, and it was on sale, too!

72

*try—tried
buy—bought

Community Connections

Work with a group of students to complete the following guide to your community. Compare your guide with other groups' guides. Then "publish" a community guide as a class.

Community Guide

The Best Restaurant . . . .

The Best Department Store . . . .

The Best Newspaper . . . .

The Most Interesting Tourist Sight . . . .

The Best TV Channel . . . .

The Most Exciting Place . . . .

Interview

Fill out the following Opinion Survey. Then interview other students in your class and people in your community. Write down people's opinions and then report your findings to the class. Compare everybody's opinions.

Opinion Survey

1. Who is the best actor?
. . . .

2. Who is the best actress?
. . . .

3. What is the best television program?
. . . .

4. What are the most nutritious foods?
. . . .

5. What is the best form of exercise?
. . . .

6. What is the most dangerous sport?
. . . .

buy stamps at the post office
take the kids to the zoo tomorrow

A. You know . . . I think we should stop at the bank.

B. Why? Do we need cash?

A. Yes. Remember . . . We have to buy stamps at the post office, and we're going to take the kids to the zoo tomorrow.

B. You're right. I forgot. How much do you think we should get?

A. I think forty dollars ($40) will be enough.

B. I think so, too.

1 buy food for the weekend
see a movie tonight

2 pay the baby-sitter
go out for dinner
tomorrow night

3 buy a birthday present
for Uncle Bob
drive to the beach
tomorrow

4 get an anniversary gift
for your parents
visit my sister in New
York on Sunday

5 get more dog food
for Rover
go skiing this weekend

You need to stop at the bank to get some cash.

Fill It In!

Fill in the correct word.

 **has to** • **have to** • **had to**

1. We _have to_ buy a gift for Uncle Charlie this weekend.
2. Ellen can't go to the movies with us because she _____ baby-sit this Friday night.
3. I'm afraid you'll _____ drive. I don't have my license with me.
4. Did your friends _____ stop at the bank to get cash?
5. I _____ do my homework last night.
6. Do you _____ buy a crib for the baby?
7. Timmy can't play with you this morning. He _____ help me do some things around the house.
8. Unfortunately, I won't be at your party tonight. I _____ work overtime.

REFLECTIONS
Do you use a lot of cash during the week? What do you pay for in cash? How much do you usually pay for these things?

Discuss in pairs or small groups, and then share your ideas with the class.

CrossTalk

I'm going to see a movie.

My boyfriend and I are going to go skating.

My wife and I are going to take our kids to the beach.

Talk with a partner about what you're going to do this weekend. Share your weekend plans with the rest of the class and decide who's going to have the most exciting weekend.

Your Turn

For Writing and Discussion

Fill in the amounts of money you think are appropriate, and then compare with what other students in the class think.

To get some gas and go out for dinner, it'll cost . . . .

To see a movie and go out for a snack, I'll need . . . .

To go to a laundromat and then to a ballgame, it'll cost . . . .

To get the best tickets for the rock concert, I'll need . . . .

To buy a birthday present for my (wife/husband/best friend), I'll need . . . .

To have a party for my friends, I'll need to write a check for . . . .

A. I'd like to deposit this in my savings account.
B. All right. Please print your name on the deposit slip.
A. Oh. Did I forget to print my name on the deposit slip?
B. Yes, you did.
A. Sorry.

Fill It In!

account	cash	checking	number	slip
amount	check	endorse	print	withdrawal

1 I should cash this ___check___ soon.

2 Would you please write the account _____?

3 Don't sign your name. Please _____ it.

4 Please sign your name on the _____ slip.

5 I'd like to deposit this in my _____ account.

6 I deposited my paycheck in my _____.

7 I'm sorry. Did I forget to _____ the check?

8 I need to _____ my paycheck.

9 Sign the withdrawal _____.

10 Write the total _____ of the deposit here.

George Goes to the Bank

Choose the correct answer.

George B. Best	CASH	
470 Fifth Street	CHECKS	150.00
Elm City, OH		10.00
		220.50
Date _September 3_ 19 _99_		
George B. Best	TOTAL	380.50
Sign here ONLY if cash received from deposit	Less cash received	50.00
Account #: 49327 0 3095 049	Total Deposit	330.50

1 George Best is ____.
- a. writing a check
- (b.) putting money in the bank
- c. withdrawing money

2 He went to the bank ____.
- a. yesterday
- b. on September 3
- c. on Fifth Street

3 The total amount of the checks is ____.
- a. $330.50
- b. $380.50
- c. $50.00

4 He wants to receive ____ in cash.
- a. $50.00
- b. $380.00
- c. $330.50

REFLECTIONS
Do you use a bank? What kind of account do you have? What services does your bank offer? Are there differences between banks in different countries you know? What are the differences?

5 His total deposit is ____.
- a. $50.00
- b. $330.50
- c. $380.50

6 His account number is ____.
- a. not on the deposit slip
- b. $330.50
- c. 49327 0 3095 049

7 He signed the deposit slip because ____.
- a. he wanted to receive some cash
- b. you're always supposed to sign it
- c. he deposited a lot of money

Discuss in pairs or small groups, and then share your ideas with the class.

A. What are you doing?

B. I'm balancing the checkbook.

A. Oh. I forgot to tell you. I wrote a check to Dr. Anderson for Billy's examination.

B. Oh. Do you remember the amount?

A. Yes. Seventy-five dollars ($75).

B. Okay. Thanks.

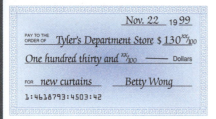

1

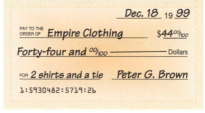

2

3

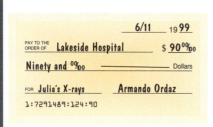

4

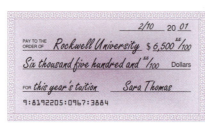

5

Your husband or wife is balancing the checkbook, and you just remembered a check you wrote.

Matching Lines

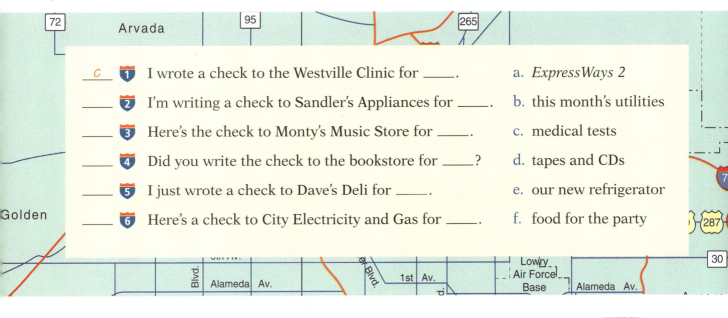

72 | Arvada | 95 | 265

_c_ **1** I wrote a check to the Westville Clinic for ____.

2 I'm writing a check to Sandler's Appliances for ____.

3 Here's the check to Monty's Music Store for ____.

4 Did you write the check to the bookstore for ____?

5 I just wrote a check to Dave's Deli for ____.

6 Here's a check to City Electricity and Gas for ____.

a. _ExpressWays 2_

b. this month's utilities

c. medical tests

d. tapes and CDs

e. our new refrigerator

f. food for the party

Golden

Blvd. | Alameda Av. | 1st Av. | Lowry Air Force Base | Alameda Av. | 30

Listen

Listen to each conversation and decide which check the people are talking about.

May 5, 19 99
PAY TO THE ORDER OF City Hospital $ 112.00
One hundred twelve and 00/100 ——— Dollars
FOR examination   Charles Lee
4:6830921:8922:51

____

Sept. 21, 20 01
PAY TO THE ORDER OF University Bookstore $ 50.00
Fifty and 00/100 ——— Dollars
FOR books   Linda Wilson
1:5930482:5719:26

1

Feb. 15, 19 99
PAY TO THE ORDER OF Elm City $ 27.00
Twenty-seven and 00/100 ——— Dollars
FOR water & trash   Don Williams
1:4618793:4503:42

____

May 16, 20 02
PAY TO THE ORDER OF City University $ 150.00
One hundred fifty and 00/100 ——— Dollars
FOR tuition   Richard White
8:3047289:4493:99

____

Jan. 31, 19 99
PAY TO THE ORDER OF Better Video Co. $ 125.00
One hundred twenty-five and 00/100 ——— Dollars
FOR tapes   Robert Cole
9:8192205:0967:3884

____

Sept. 3, 20 00
PAY TO THE ORDER OF City Bookstore $ 15.00
Fifteen and 00/100 ——— Dollars
FOR books   Susan Herrera
1:7291489:124:90

____

CrossTalk

Talk with a partner about paying bills.

Who pays the bills in your household?
Does that person typically pay by check or
  by credit card?

Which credit cards do people in your family use?
Are some credit cards better to use than others? Why?

Report to the class and compare the results
of your discussions.

A. Why are you banging on the vending machine?

B. I'm trying to buy soda, but I just lost my money.

A. What did you put in?

B. Two quarters and a dime.*

A. Sixty cents? That's too bad! You should call the number on the machine and ask for your money back.

B. I will.

a penny
1 cent

a nickel
5 cents

a dime
10 cents

a quarter
25 cents

Oh, no! You just lost your money in a vending machine!

Fill It In!

Fill in the correct numbers.

A. It's 10:15. Time for a break! I'm going to get a cup of coffee. Do you want anything?

B. Sure, if you don't mind. Please get me a cup of coffee, too. That's fifty cents, right? Here are ___*two*___[1] quarters. And let's see . . . how much are the donuts?

A. Forty-five cents.

B. Okay. Could you also get me a donut? Here's _____[2] quarter, _____[3] dime, and _____[4] nickels.

A. All right.

B. Oh, one more thing! Could you also get me a bag of potato chips? They're thirty-five cents. Here's _____[5] quarter, _____[6] nickel, and _____[7] pennies.

A. Hmm. I don't think the vending machine takes pennies.

B. You're right. What can I get for thirty cents?

A. Not much these days!

Listen

Listen to the conversations and choose the correct amount.

1	a. 25 cents (circled) b. 10 cents	**4**	a. 50 cents b. 25 cents	**7**	a. 45¢ b. 55¢
2	a. 25¢ b. 35¢	**5**	a. $.55 b. $.50	**8**	a. 95 cents b. 90 cents
3	a. 50¢ b. 60¢	**6**	a. 80 cents b. 90 cents	**9**	a. $.40 b. $.30

Cultural Intersections

What are the names of bills and coins in your country? What is today's exchange rate of your country's currency?

Bring some coins and bills to class. What writing is on them? Whose pictures are on them? Why do you think these people's pictures are on your country's currency?

81

Did You Remember to Pay the Telephone Bill?

A. Did you remember to pay the telephone bill?

B. The telephone bill? That isn't due yet.

A. Are you sure?

B. Yes. I'm positive. Look! Here's the bill. It's due on January 10th.*

A. Oh, okay.

*January (JAN)	July (JUL)	1st – first	21st – twenty-first
February (FEB)	August (AUG)	2nd – second	22nd – twenty-second
March (MAR)	September (SEPT)	3rd – third	23rd – twenty-third
April (APR)	October (OCT)	4th – fourth	24th – twenty-fourth
May (MAY)	November (NOV)	5th – fifth	25th – twenty-fifth
June (JUN)	December (DEC)	•	•
		•	•
		•	•
		20th – twentieth	30th – thirtieth

You're paying your bills. Some are due now, and others aren't due yet.

Listen

What numbers do you hear?

1 a. 16th
  b. 13th

4 a. 26th
  b. 21st

7 a. 13th
  b. 30th

10 a. 14th
  b. 4th

2 a. 21st
  b. 25th

5 a. 22nd
  b. 27th

8 a. 1st
  b. 30th

11 a. 1st
  b. 21st

3 a. 1st
  b. 3rd

6 a. 12th
  b. 20th

9 a. 23rd
  b. 31st

12 a. 17th
  b. 70th

Your Turn

For Writing and Discussion

My birthday is June 9th.

My parents' anniversary is May 15th.

My favorite day of the year is . . . .

Tell about some special days in your life. Why are they special? What do you do on those days?

Cultural Intersections

Do you know when the following holidays are celebrated in the United States?

  e **1** Christmas

  ___ **2** Thanksgiving

  ___ **3** Halloween

  ___ **4** Labor Day

  ___ **5** Independence Day

  ___ **6** Valentine's Day

a. July 4th

b. February 14th

c. 1st Monday in September

d. 3rd Thursday in November

e. December 25th

f. October 31st

Tell students in your class what you know about these holidays. If you want to know more, look in an encyclopedia and report to the class what you learned about these U.S. celebrations.

Now tell the dates of important holidays in YOUR country. How do you celebrate these holidays?

INTERCHANGE

I Think There's a Mistake on My Electric Bill

A. Southeast Electric Company. May I help you?

B. Yes. I think there's a mistake on my electric bill.

A. Oh. What's the problem?

B. I believe I was charged too much.

A. I see. What is your name?

B. John Lawson.

A. And your account number?

B. 463 21 0978.

A. And what is the amount on your bill?

B. Four hundred and thirty dollars ($430).

A. All right. Please hold, and I'll check our records.

B. Thank you.

A. _____. May I help you?

B. Yes. I think there's a mistake on my _____ bill.

A. Oh. What's the problem?

B. I believe I was charged too much.

A. I see. What is your name?

B. _____.

A. And your account number?

B. _____.

A. And what is the amount on your bill?

B. _____.

A. All right. Please hold, and I'll check our records.

B. Thank you.

There is a mistake on one of your utility bills (electric, gas, telephone, oil, water, cable TV). Call the company and tell them about the mistake, using the model dialog above as a guide. Feel free to adapt and expand the model any way you wish.

Reading: *Bob Anderson and His Checkbook*

Every Saturday morning, Bob Anderson sits down at his kitchen table with a cup of coffee, his checkbook, a calculator, a notebook, and the bills he received during the week. This week, Bob has to pay four bills. The mortgage payment on his house is due. He also has to pay the monthly car payment, the electric bill, and a credit card bill. The credit card bill is always the biggest bill of the month.

Bob is very careful when he writes the checks. He always checks the information when he finishes. Is the date right? Is the amount correct? Did he spell everything right? Did he remember to write the account number on the check? Did he sign the check?

Bob balances his checkbook after every check he writes. He enters information in his check register: the number of the check, the date, the name of the person or company, and the amount. He uses his calculator and makes sure that he knows the correct balance of his checking account. He wants to be sure that the balance is exact. He doesn't want to make even the smallest mistake.

Then Bob writes in his notebook. The notebook helps him keep his monthly budget. Bob writes down the amount he spends each month on housing, utilities, food, clothing, entertainment, and other expenses. In this way, he knows exactly how much he can add to his savings account.

Bob is trying to save a lot of money this year. He wants to go back to school in September, and tuition will be very expensive. That's why he spends every Saturday morning at his kitchen table with his checkbook.

What's the Answer?

1. Bob Anderson pays his bills _____.
   a. with a calculator
   b. on Saturday mornings   *(b circled)*
2. The mortgage check is for _____.
   a. the car
   b. the house
3. The check with the largest amount goes to _____.
   a. the credit card company
   b. the bank
4. Bob has to remember to _____ the check.
   a. sign
   b. finish
5. He doesn't want to _____.
   a. make any mistakes
   b. be sure the balance is correct

6. He _____ the information in his check register.
   a. goes into
   b. writes
7. Bob uses a notebook to _____.
   a. know his checking account balance
   b. keep a budget
8. Bob writes in his notebook _____.
   a. how much he spends at the supermarket
   b. clothing he needs to buy
9. He's saving money because _____.
   a. the credit card bill is always large
   b. school costs a lot
10. Bob is probably _____.
    a. very careful
    b. not very accurate

85

☐ **Furniture**
armchair
bookcase
crib
kitchen table
mattress
rug
sofa

☐ **Department Store Items**
cassette player
computer
stereo system
typewriter

☐ **Household Appliances**
air conditioner
refrigerator

☐ **Describing**
attractive
big
comfortable
expensive
firm
good
large
lightweight
modern
nice
powerful
quiet

☐ **Finances**
afford
balance
buy
pay

cash
check
checkbook
money

☐ **Banking**
cash *this* check
deposit
endorse
make a withdrawal
print *your name*
sign *your name*
account number
amount

check
checking account
deposit slip
savings account
withdrawal slip

☐ **Coins**
penny – 1 cent
nickel – 5 cents
dime – 10 cents
quarter – 25 cents

☐ **Utility Bills**
cable TV bill
electric bill
gas bill
oil bill
telephone bill
water bill

account number
amount
due

☐ **Months of the Year**
January (JAN)
February (FEB)
March (MAR)
April (APR)
May (MAY)
June (JUN)
July (JUL)
August (AUG)
September (SEPT)
October (OCT)
November (NOV)
December (DEC)

Now Leaving Exit 4 Construction Area

☐ **Adjectives**
☐ **Comparatives**
☐ **Superlatives**
☐ **Review:**
   Future: Going to
   Have to
   Should

Sorry for the inconvenience. For more information see page 172.

ExpressWays Checklist

I can . . .

☐ evaluate the affordability of items in a store
☐ budget my money
☐ accomplish everyday banking procedures
☐ discuss balancing a checkbook
☐ understand denominations of money
☐ evaluate payment of household bills
☐ deal effectively with errors on household bills

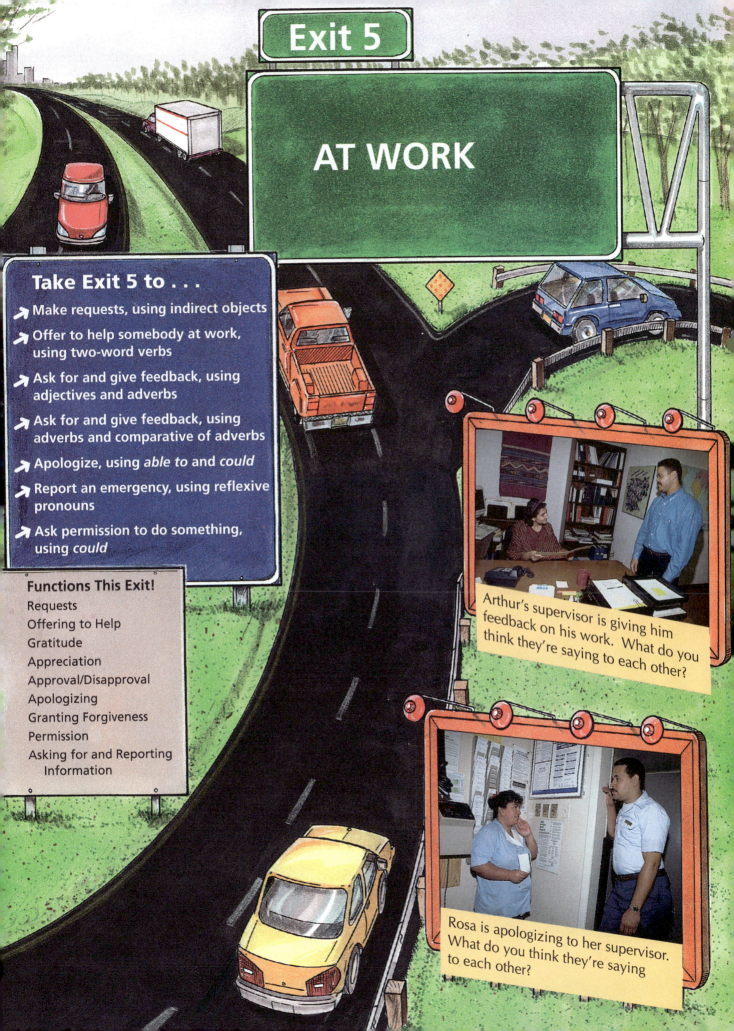

Exit 5

AT WORK

Take Exit 5 to . . .

➔ Make requests, using indirect objects

➔ Offer to help somebody at work, using two-word verbs

➔ Ask for and give feedback, using adjectives and adverbs

➔ Ask for and give feedback, using adverbs and comparative of adverbs

➔ Apologize, using *able to* and *could*

➔ Report an emergency, using reflexive pronouns

➔ Ask permission to do something, using *could*

Functions This Exit!

Requests
Offering to Help
Gratitude
Appreciation
Approval/Disapproval
Apologizing
Granting Forgiveness
Permission
Asking for and Reporting Information

Arthur's supervisor is giving him feedback on his work. What do you think they're saying to each other?

Rosa is apologizing to her supervisor. What do you think they're saying to each other?

A. Could you please give this report to Mr. Lewis?

B. Certainly. I'll give him the report right away.

A. Thank you.

B. My pleasure.

Constructions Ahead!

> Please **give** this report **to Mr. Lewis**.
> I'll **give him** the report right away.

1 Please mail this letter to Mrs. Carter.

Of course. I'll ___mail___ ___her___ the letter right away.

2 Please write a memo to all our customers.

Certainly. I'll _____ _____ the memo this afternoon.

3 Will you please send this package to Mr. Wong?

Certainly. I'll _____ _____ the package immediately.

4 Can you fax this note to my wife?

Of course. I'll _____ _____ the note right away.

5 Walter? Can you read a bedtime story to the children?

Sure. I'll _____ _____ a story right now.

Listen

Listen and write the number under the correct picture.

_____   _____   ___1___   _____   _____

CrossTalk

Talk with a partner about the ways you communicate with people you know.

Do you call people on the telephone?
Do you write letters?
Do you use a computer?
Do you use a fax machine?
Do you use e-mail?

Which is the fastest way? the easiest way? the most convenient way?
Which do you enjoy the most?

Would You Like Me to Set Up the Conference Room?

set up the conference room?

A. Would you like me to set up the conference room?

B. Sure. If you don't mind.

A. Not at all. I'd be happy to set it up.

B. Thanks. I really appreciate it.

1 give out the reports?

2 hang up these signs?

3 put away the dishes?

4 clean up the supply room?

5 take down the Christmas decorations?

Offer to help someone at work.

Fill It In!

Fill in the correct words.

| take down | set up | put away | hang up | give out | clean up |

1. I'll be happy to __give__ __out__ the paychecks.

Thanks. Can you __give__ them __out__ right away?

2. Do you want me to _____ _____ the supply room? It's really a mess!

Sure. _____ _____ _____ anytime today.

3. Would you like me to _____ _____ the room for today's meeting?

No, that's okay. I can _____ _____ _____ later.

4. Do you want me to _____ _____ these "For Sale" signs? The sale starts tomorrow.

Yes, please. _____ _____ _____ over there.

5. Do you want me to _____ _____ those "For Sale" signs? The sale was over yesterday.

Good idea! You should _____ _____ _____ right away.

6. I'll be happy to _____ _____ those clean glasses.

Thanks. Please _____ _____ _____ right now.

InterActions

People are very helpful at work today! In pairs or small groups, decide on a workplace. For example:

an office

a hotel

a factory

a restaurant

a mechanic's garage

Create situations in which workers are offering to help their co-workers. Present your role plays to the class. Can other students guess where the conversations are taking place?

You're a Very Accurate Translator!

accurate translator

A. You're a very accurate translator!

B. Do you really think so?

A. Absolutely! You're translating very accurately!

B. Thank you for saying so.

1 graceful dancer

2 neat worker

3 careful painter

4 good* typist

5 fast* assembler

Express your approval of someone's work.

*good—well
fast—fast

Constructions Ahead!

accurate – accurately	good – well
graceful – gracefully	fast – fast
careful – carefully	
neat – neatly	

1 Doris does her work very ____.
  a. neat
  (b.) neatly

2 You're typing very ____.
  a. accurate
  b. accurately

3 Michael is an excellent painter.
He paints very ____.
  a. careful
  b. carefully

4 I'm a very ____ worker.
  a. fast
  b. neatly

5 Mrs. Wu is a very good teacher.
She teaches very ____.
  a. good
  b. well

6 Alex is a very ____ assembler.
  a. fast
  b. fastly

7 You really dance ____!
  a. graceful
  b. gracefully

8 You're a very ____ typist!
  a. accurately
  b. good

Listen

Listen and decide whether the following statements are true or false.

 REFLECTIONS
How do you feel when somebody tells you you're doing something well? Why do you think it's important for people to get *positive feedback*?

1 a. True
  (b.) False

2 a. True
  b. False

3 a. True
  b. False

4 a. True
  b. False

5 a. True
  b. False

6 a. True
  b. False

Discuss in pairs or small groups, and then share your ideas with the class.

CrossTalk

What are some work activities you do well? Talk with a partner and then tell the class.
Create a master list of everybody's workplace skills.

A. Am I typing fast enough?

B. Actually, you should try to type faster.

A. Oh, okay. I'll try. Thanks for telling me.

A. Am I painting carefully enough?

B. Actually, you should try to paint more carefully.

A. Oh, okay. I'll try. Thanks for telling me.

1

2

3

4

5

Ask how well you're doing your job.

*loud or loudly

94

Constructions Ahead!

fast – faster	**quickly – quicker**
loud(ly) – louder	**slowly – slower**

carefully – more carefully   **well – better**
politely – more politely

1 Am I working fast enough?

Actually, you're supposed to work ___faster___.

2 Your next-door neighbor is playing his violin very loudly tonight!

Believe it or not, he played it even _____ last night!

3 Roger read the instructions carefully, but he still made a lot of mistakes!

You know, he should read them again even _____.

4 You didn't do your homework very well last night.

I'll do it _____ tonight.

5 Children these days don't speak very politely to their teachers.

I agree. Parents should really teach their children to speak _____.

6 Those workers are loading that truck very quickly!

You're right. They're loading it _____ than they should. They're breaking the boxes!

Listen

Listen and choose the correct word.

1 a. accurate
   b.) accurately

3 a. politely
   b. more politely

5 a. faster
   b. louder

2 a. careful
   b. carefully

4 a. well
   b. good

6 a. slower
   b. quicker

REFLECTIONS
How do you want to improve? What things do you think you should do better?

Discuss in pairs or small groups, and then share your ideas with the class.

Community Connections

Be an observer! Visit a work site in your community and evaluate the following:

Are people working quickly or slowly?
Are workers speaking politely to customers?

Report your findings to the class and compare with other students' observations.

attend a wedding out of town

work this weekend

A. I'm really sorry, but I won't be able to work this weekend.

B. Oh? Why not?

A. I have to attend a wedding out of town.

B. No problem. It's okay.

go to a meeting

1. pick up Mr. Lee at the airport.

go to the doctor

2. type the annual report today

meet with the boss

3. see your presentation

leave work early today

4. stay until the end of the meeting

unload the delivery truck

5. set up the conference room

Apologize for something at work you won't be able to do.

take my daughter to the doctor

work overtime yesterday

A. I'm sorry that I $\left\{ \begin{array}{l} \text{couldn't} \\ \text{wasn't able to} \end{array} \right\}$ work overtime yesterday.

B. That's all right.

A. The reason is that I had to take my daughter to the doctor.

B. I understand. Don't worry about it.

go to the dentist

pick up my wife at the airport

go to a meeting at my son's school

1 come in early today

2 help you take inventory on Saturday

3 finish the report yesterday afternoon

welcome a visitor from China

meet with the Swiss ambassador

4 come to the meeting this morning

5 attend your press conference

Apologize for something at work you weren't able to do.

Constructions Ahead!

| I / He / She / It / We / You / They | will/won't be able to | I / He / She / It | was/wasn't able to | work. |
| | | We / You / They | were/weren't able to | |

| I / He / She / It / We / You / They | could/couldn't work. |

1. Michael <u>won't</u> <u>be</u> <u>able</u> <u>to</u> come to work tomorrow. He has to go to the dentist.

2. Carla _____ work yesterday because she was sick.

3. I'm sorry we _____ _____ _____ come to your party last weekend. We were out of town.

4. I'm sorry I _____ _____ _____ be at the meeting yesterday. The reason is I _____ start my car.

5. _____ you be _____ _____ work late tonight?

6. We're sorry we _____ stay for the presentation, but we had to meet with our supervisor.

7. _____ you _____ _____ go to the meeting yesterday? I _____ _____ _____ be there. I had to finish the annual report.

8. I'm really sorry I _____ finish the report yesterday afternoon, Mrs. Applebee. I had to leave work early. But I'll _____ _____ _____ finish it this afternoon.

InterView

Interview students in your class and ask their opinions of the following excuses. Are they good excuses or poor excuses for not being able to do something at work?

I have to . . .	good excuse	poor excuse
• take my son to the doctor.	_____	_____
• go to a meeting at my son's school.	_____	_____
• play tennis.	_____	_____
• get my car fixed.	_____	_____
• meet with my daughter's teacher.	_____	_____
• clean my house because my relatives are coming to visit.	_____	_____
• shop for food.	_____	_____
• go to the dentist.	_____	_____

Also, ask each student to think of one other good excuse and one other poor excuse. Make a list on the board and compare everybody's responses.

Reading: *Too Many Excuses!*

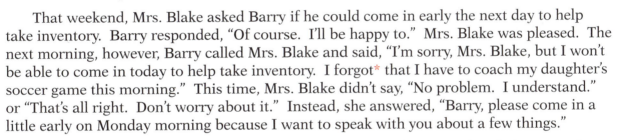

Barry Winter is a salesperson in the Men's Clothing Department at the Omni Department Store. A few weeks ago Barry's supervisor, Mrs. Blake, asked him to work overtime because the store had to prepare for a big sale. Barry told Mrs. Blake that he couldn't work overtime because he had to pick up his son at school. Mrs. Blake said* to Barry, "No problem. I understand."

A few days after that, Barry went into Mrs. Blake's office and asked, "Can I possibly leave early today? I have a doctor's appointment." Mrs. Blake replied, "Of course. Don't worry about it." And so Barry left work early that day, even though the store was very busy and some other employees were out sick.

The next week, Mrs. Blake came over to Barry and said, "Can I ask you a favor? There's going to be a large shipment of new clothing, and we need some salespeople to help us unload it." Barry told Mrs. Blake that he was sorry, but he wasn't able to help because he was having problems with his back.

That weekend, Mrs. Blake asked Barry if he could come in early the next day to help take inventory. Barry responded, "Of course. I'll be happy to." Mrs. Blake was pleased. The next morning, however, Barry called Mrs. Blake and said, "I'm sorry, Mrs. Blake, but I won't be able to come in today to help take inventory. I forgot* that I have to coach my daughter's soccer game this morning." This time, Mrs. Blake didn't say, "No problem. I understand." or "That's all right. Don't worry about it." Instead, she answered, "Barry, please come in a little early on Monday morning because I want to speak with you about a few things."

Barry replied, "I'm sorry, Mrs. Blake, but I won't be able to come in early because I have to take my car to the mechanic. But I'll be able to speak with you at the beginning of the work day." Mrs. Blake said "Good-bye" and hung up* the phone.

CrossTalk

Talk with a partner about Barry Winter's behavior.

What's your opinion? Is he a "cooperative employee"?
Did he give too many excuses to his supervisor?

Share your thoughts with other students in the class.

InterActions

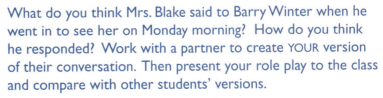

What do you think Mrs. Blake said to Barry Winter when he went in to see her on Monday morning? How do you think he responded? Work with a partner to create YOUR version of their conversation. Then present your role play to the class and compare with other students' versions.

*say—said
forget—forgot
hang up—hung up

Martha cut* herself, and she's bleeding very badly!

A. You won't believe what happened!

B. What happened?

A. Martha cut herself, and she's bleeding very badly!

B. Tell her to press on the cut! I'll call the doctor!

1 Rocco burned himself on the stove!

2 Carla hurt herself on her machine!

3 I poked myself in the eye!

4 Sally and I cut ourselves in Biology lab!

5 Bob and Tim spilled soup all over themselves!

Report an emergency at work or at school.

*cut–cut

Constructions Ahead!

I		myself.
You		yourself.
He		himself.
She	hurt	herself.
It		itself.
We		ourselves.
You		yourselves.
They		themselves.

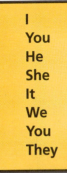

REFLECTIONS
Is there a first-aid kit at your school or at your job? What kinds of accidents and injuries can happen at school or at work? How can people prevent these accidents and injuries?

Discuss in pairs or small groups, and then share your ideas with the class.

1 Oh, no! Did you hurt ___yourself___?

2 I feel terrible. My husband cut _____ at work today!

3 I burned _____ very badly!

4 Believe it or not, we painted our house _____!

5 You two are going to hurt _____! Be careful!

6 My daughter just poked _____ in the eye!

7 Two employees in our office cut _____ this morning.

8 Our parrot talks to _____ all the time!

CrossTalk

What's your opinion? What should you do when . . .

someone burns himself or herself?

someone eats something harmful?

someone gets an electrical shock?

someone gets hit by a car?

someone cuts himself or herself?

Discuss with a partner and then share your "emergency solutions" with the class.

101

INTERCHANGE

Could I Possibly Leave an Hour Early Today?

A. Excuse me, Mrs. Lopez.

B. Yes?

A. Could I possibly leave an hour early today?

B. Hmm. Well, I'm not really sure.

A. The reason I'm asking is my wife hurt herself at work and I have to take her to the doctor.

B. Well, in that case, of course you can leave an hour early today.

A. Thank you very much.

A. Excuse me, (Mr./Mrs./Ms./Miss) _____.

B. Yes?

A. Could I possibly _____?

B. Hmm. Well, I'm not really sure.

A. The reason I'm asking is _____
_____.

B. Well, in that case, of course you can _____.

A. Thank you very much.

You're asking your employer for permission to do something. Create an original conversation, using the model dialog above as a guide. Feel free to adapt and expand the model any way you wish.

Match the People and the Conversations

Read the following conversations between employees and supervisors. Then match the conversation with what one of the people is thinking.

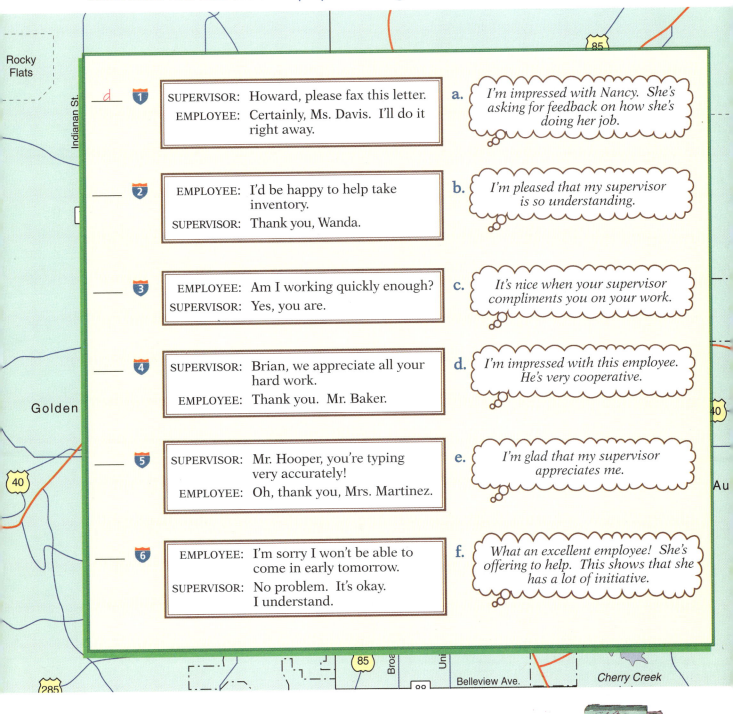

d **1**
SUPERVISOR: Howard, please fax this letter.
EMPLOYEE: Certainly, Ms. Davis. I'll do it right away.

a. *I'm impressed with Nancy. She's asking for feedback on how she's doing her job.*

2
EMPLOYEE: I'd be happy to help take inventory.
SUPERVISOR: Thank you, Wanda.

b. *I'm pleased that my supervisor is so understanding.*

3
EMPLOYEE: Am I working quickly enough?
SUPERVISOR: Yes, you are.

c. *It's nice when your supervisor compliments you on your work.*

4
SUPERVISOR: Brian, we appreciate all your hard work.
EMPLOYEE: Thank you. Mr. Baker.

d. *I'm impressed with this employee. He's very cooperative.*

5
SUPERVISOR: Mr. Hooper, you're typing very accurately!
EMPLOYEE: Oh, thank you, Mrs. Martinez.

e. *I'm glad that my supervisor appreciates me.*

6
EMPLOYEE: I'm sorry I won't be able to come in early tomorrow.
SUPERVISOR: No problem. It's okay. I understand.

f. *What an excellent employee! She's offering to help. This shows that she has a lot of initiative.*

Your Turn

For Writing and Discussion

In your opinion, what are some qualities of a good employee?
What are some qualities of a good supervisor?

Looking Back

☐ Objects on the Job
announcement
dishes
first-aid kit
letter
memo
note
package
report
sign

☐ Job Procedures
clean up *the supply room*
fax *this memo*
give out *the reports*
hang up *these signs*
mail *this letter*
put away *the dishes*
set up *the conference room*
take inventory
take down *the decorations*

☐ Job Injuries
burn *himself*
cut *herself*
hurt *herself*
poke *myself*
spill

☐ Occupations
assembler
dancer
painter
translator
typist
worker

☐ Additional Employment Vocabulary
annual report
conference room
customer
delivery truck
feedback
initiative
meeting
overtime
paycheck
presentation
supervisor
supply room

☐ Feedback on Job Performance
accurate – accurately
careful – carefully
fast – fast
good – well
graceful – gracefully
loud – loud(ly)
neat – neatly
polite – politely
quick – quickly
slow – slowly

Now Leaving Exit 5 Construction Area

☐ **Indirect Objects**
☐ **Two-Word Verbs**
☐ **Able to**
☐ **Could**
☐ **Adverbs**
☐ **Comparative of Adverbs**
☐ **Reflexive Pronouns**

Sorry for the inconvenience. For more information see pages 173 and 174.

ExpressWays Checklist

I can . . .
☐ make requests at work
☐ offer to help somebody
☐ ask for and give feedback
☐ apologize
☐ report an emergency
☐ ask permission to do something

Exit 6

RULES AND REGULATIONS

Take Exit 6 to . . .

↗ Ask about and tell people what they aren't allowed to do, using impersonal expressions with *you*

↗ Understand traffic signs

↗ Understand traffic violations, using the past tense and the past continuous tense

↗ Understand rules of an apartment building, using impersonal expressions with *you*

↗ Deal effectively with housing problems, using *going to* and *will*

↗ Understand rules and regulations at work sites, using *must*

↗ Express opinions about issues that concern you, using *should* and *ought to*

Functions This Exit!

Permission
Asking for and Reporting Information
Surprise–Disbelief
Promising
Focusing Attention
Checking and Indicating Understanding
Initiating a Topic

A police officer just stopped Edward. What do you think the police officer and Edward are saying to each other?

The owner of this apartment building is explaining the rules of the building to a new tenant. What do you think they're saying to each other?

A. Are you allowed to swim here?

B. Yes, you are.

A. Thanks.

A. Are you allowed to smoke here?

B. No, you aren't.

A. Oh, okay. Thanks.

Ask if you're allowed to do something.

ExpressWays

1. Are you allowed to swim here?
Yes, you are.

2. Are you allowed to smoke here?
_____

3. Are you allowed to camp here?
_____

4. Are you allowed to fish here?
_____

5. Are you allowed to ice skate on this lake?
_____

6. Are you allowed to park here?
_____

Listen

Listen and choose the correct sign.

_____ _____ _____ _____ 1 _____

CrossTalk

Talk with a partner about rules and regulations in public places in your city or town:

in your neighborhood   on public transportation
in public parks and playgrounds   in stores

Compare your list with other students' lists.

park

A. Excuse me. You aren't allowed to park here.

B. Oh?

A. Yes. There's the sign.

B. Hmm. "Parking for Handicapped Only." I didn't see the sign. Thanks for telling me.

A. You're welcome.

1. smoke

2. walk

3. stand

4. come in

5. eat

Tell somebody that something isn't allowed.

Match the Signs

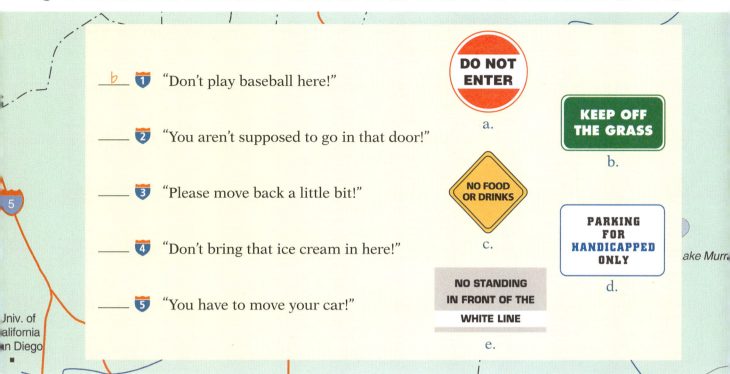

_b_ **1** "Don't play baseball here!"

_____ **2** "You aren't supposed to go in that door!"

_____ **3** "Please move back a little bit!"

_____ **4** "Don't bring that ice cream in here!"

_____ **5** "You have to move your car!"

DO NOT ENTER
a.

KEEP OFF THE GRASS
b.

NO FOOD OR DRINKS
c.

PARKING FOR HANDICAPPED ONLY
d.

NO STANDING IN FRONT OF THE WHITE LINE
e.

Listen

Listen and decide where each of these conversations is taking place.

1 a. in a hospital
   b. on the telephone

2 a. in a library
   b. in a shoe store

3 a. in a restaurant
   b. on a bus

4 a. in a park
   b. in a parking lot

5 a. in a car
   b. in an office

6 a. in a supermarket
   b. at a lake

7 a. at a lake or in a park
   b. in a women's bathroom

8 a. in a cafeteria
   b. in a museum

Community Connections

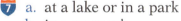

Go out into your community with your notebook and copy down warnings on signs that you see — for example, in public buildings, on public transportation, and on the street. Compare your list with other students' lists and compile a master list of signs in your community.

InterActions

For fun, work with one or more students to create role plays based on the signs you discovered in Community Connections above. Present your "dramas" to the class.

109

A. Oh, my goodness!*

B. What's the matter?

A. Didn't you see the sign?

B. The sign? No. What did it say?

A. "No Right Turn on Red."

B. "No Right Turn on Red"?!

A. Yes.

B. Oh, my goodness!*

STOP

DO NOT ENTER

NO LEFT TURN

1

2

3

ONE WAY

NO U TURN

Oh, my goodness! You didn't see a traffic sign!

4

5

*Oh, my goodness!
 Oops!
 Uh-oh!

Match the Signs

_c_ 🛡1 "You aren't allowed to turn around here!"

___ 🛡2 "Don't turn left!"

___ 🛡3 "You can't make a right turn on a red light!"

___ 🛡4 "That street goes in only one direction!"

___ 🛡5 "You aren't supposed to go there!"

___ 🛡6 "You have to stop here!"

STOP
a.

DO NOT ENTER
b.

c.

NO RIGHT TURN ON RED
d.

e.

ONE WAY
f.

Listen

Listen to the conversation and choose the correct conclusion.

🛡1 a. He made* a U turn.
    b. He'll make a U turn.

🛡2 a. He's a good driver.
    b. He didn't stop.

🛡3 a. The driver saw* the sign.
    b. The driver made a wrong turn.

🛡4 a. He made a wrong turn.
    b. He wasn't sure.

🛡5 a. He wants a ticket.
    b. He's getting a ticket.

🛡6 a. He forgot to turn around.
    b. He's driving in the wrong direction.

Community Connections

Go out again into the community and this time look for as many different driving and traffic signs as you can find. For each sign:

    Write down what the sign says.
    Copy down any symbol or diagram that appears
       on the sign.

Compare with other students. Who found the most signs?

*make–made

111

A. Let me see your license.

B. Here you are, Officer. What did I do wrong?

A. You were speeding.

B. I was speeding?

A. Yes. I'm going to have to give you a ticket.

B. Oh.

Constructions Ahead!

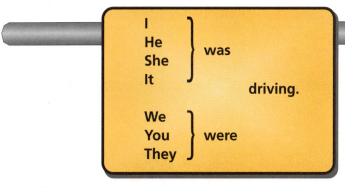

	I / He / She / It	was	
			driving.
	We / You / They	were	

| drive | rain | speed | study | talk |

1. What were you doing wrong? I *was driving* 75 miles per hour.

2. What were we doing wrong? We _____ during the test.

3. What was Martha doing wrong? She _____ on the wrong side of the road.

4. What were Bob and Susan doing when you called? They _____ for a test.

5. How was the weather for your picnic? Terrible. It _____.

6. What did I do wrong, Officer? You _____.

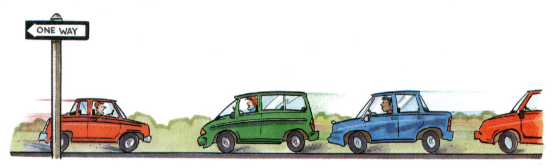

7. Why did the police officer give Stanley a ticket? He _____ the wrong way down a one-way street.

Your Turn

For Writing and Discussion

Tell about a time a police officer stopped YOU!

Why did the officer stop you?
Did you go through a red light?
Were you speeding?
What did the police officer say?
What did you say to the police officer?
Did you get a ticket?
How did you feel?

REFLECTIONS
Are there differences between police officers in different countries you know? How are they different?

Discuss in pairs or small groups, and then share your ideas with the class.

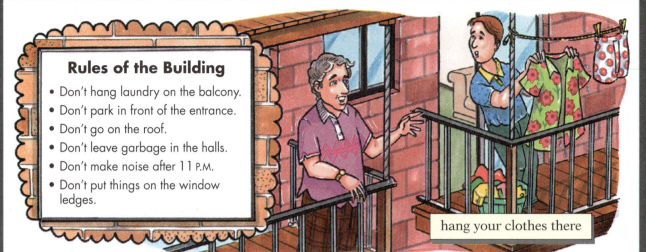

Rules of the Building

- Don't hang laundry on the balcony.
- Don't park in front of the entrance.
- Don't go on the roof.
- Don't leave garbage in the halls.
- Don't make noise after 11 P.M.
- Don't put things on the window ledges.

hang your clothes there

A. Excuse me, but I don't think you're allowed to hang your clothes there.

B. Oh?

A. Yes. Tenants aren't permitted to hang laundry on the balcony. It's one of the rules of the building.

B. Oh. I didn't know that. Sorry.

A. That's okay.

1. leave your car here

2. put up that TV antenna

3. put your garbage there

4. play your stereo so loud at this hour

5. put flowerpots there

Tell a tenant of your apartment building that what the person is doing isn't allowed.

Fill It In!

Fill in the correct word.

balcony	entrance	garbage	tenants
building	hall	window ledge	noise

1 I'm sorry. You aren't permitted to cook on the ___balcony___.

2 Don't leave those flowerpots on the _____.

3 You can pick me up at the _____ to the building.

4 Did you meet the new _____?

5 You aren't allowed to leave the _____ there.

6 Which _____ do you live in?

7 I left the packages in the _____.

8 Those people upstairs are making too much _____!

Listen

Listen to the conversations and put the number next to the rule being broken.

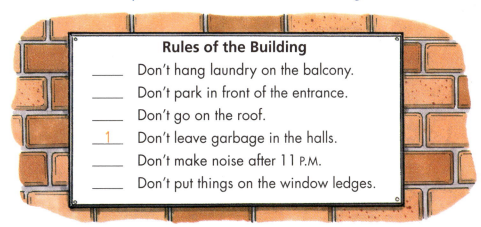

Rules of the Building

____ Don't hang laundry on the balcony.

____ Don't park in front of the entrance.

____ Don't go on the roof.

_1_ Don't leave garbage in the halls.

____ Don't make noise after 11 P.M.

____ Don't put things on the window ledges.

InterActions

You are the owner of an apartment building. Complete the following list of rules of your building. Then create a role play with one or more students who are "tenants" of your building.

Rules of the Building

....

....

....

....

....

....

....

REFLECTIONS
What kind of rules are there where you live? Do you agree with the rules?

Discuss in pairs or small groups, and then share your ideas with the class.

fix my sink

call the Health Department

Mr. Willis in Apartment 2

A. Hello. This is Mr. Willis in Apartment 2.

B. Yes? What can I do for you?

A. I'm wondering . . . When are you going to fix my sink?

B. Well, Mr. Willis, I'm very busy right now. I'll try to fix it soon.

A. You know, you promised to fix it several weeks ago. I'm afraid I'm going to have to call the Health Department.

B. Now, Mr. Willis. I'm sure that won't be necessary. I promise I'll fix your sink this week.

A. Thank you very much.

repair our toilet

call the Housing Authority

turn on our heat

call City Hall

return our security deposit

go to court

1 Mrs. Lee in Apartment 9F

2 Bill Franklin in Building 4

3 Anita Davis, who lived in Apartment 6D

spray our apartment

call the Health Department

remove the lead paint in our kitchen

contact Channel 7 News

You're upset! Call the superintendent of your apartment building and complain!

4 Ms. Rodriguez at 659 Central Avenue

5 Mr. Dempsey on the fifth floor

Promises! Promises!

1. When are you going to repair our refrigerator?

   I promise __I'll repair it__ tomorrow.

2. When are you going to paint the hallways?

   I promise _____ next week.

3. When are you going to clean up the mess on the balcony?

   I promise _____ this afternoon.

4. When are you and your sister going to take out the garbage?

   We promise _____ soon.

Matching Lines

_b_ 1. I'm going to spray ____.

____ 2. I promise I'll return ____.

____ 3. I already contacted ____.

____ 4. Tell your landlord to remove ____.

____ 5. He promises he'll turn on ____.

a. the TV station

b. your kitchen this afternoon

c. the heat

d. your security deposit soon

e. the lead paint

CrossTalk

The people on page 116 are upset. They say they're going to call the Health Department, the Housing Authority, City Hall, or a television station to complain about the housing problems they're having.

Tell about your community. What can people do if they're having these kinds of problems?

Have you ever had problems like these? What did you do about them?

117

☑ wear your uniform
☒ make the sundaes too large

A. Before you begin your new job, I'd like to tell you about two important rules here at Ike's Ice Cream Shop.

B. Yes?

A. First of all, you must always wear your uniform.

B. I understand.

A. Also, you mustn't make the sundaes too large.

B. I see.

1 ☑ wear protective glasses
☒ go into the restricted area

2 ☑ type all your reports on the computer
☒ eat at your workstation

3 ☑ greet the customers with a smile
☒ chew gum

4 ☑ punch in by 8 A.M.
☒ leave the work area without permission

5 ☑ work quickly and accurately
☒ ask too many questions

Tell a new employee about some important rules and regulations on the job.

Constructions Ahead!

| I He She It We You They | } must work. | I He She It We You They | } mustn't leave. |

Matching Lines

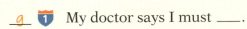

_g_ **1** My doctor says I must ___.

2 Our boss says we must ___.

3 Their teacher says they must ___.

4 My doctor says I mustn't ___.

5 Our boss says we mustn't ___.

6 His teacher says he mustn't ___.

7 Betty's landlord says she mustn't ___.

8 My landlord says I must ___.

9 The police officer said I mustn't ___.

10 I told my landlord that he must ___.

a. eat too many rich desserts

b. make noise after midnight

c. return our security deposit

d. take down my TV antenna from the roof

e. park in a "Handicapped Only" area

f. work overtime today

g. lose some weight

h. come to class late any more

i. leave the work area without permission

j. turn in their homework on time

Community Connections

Visit one or two work sites in your community.

Look for signs that tell rules and regulations.

Interview people who work there, and ask them some of the rules they must obey on the job.

Report your findings to the class and compare with what other students learned on their work site visits.

INTERCHANGE

You Should Write to the Mayor

A. You know . . . in my opinion, they should have more buses on this route in the morning.

B. Why do you say that?

A. The lines at the bus stops are long, the buses are too crowded, and people are often late for work.

B. Hmm. You should write to the mayor.*

A. Write to the mayor?

B. Yes. Really. You ought to write to the mayor and express your opinion.

A. That's a good idea. I will.

* **Some Forms of Citizen Participation**
write to/call the president
write to/call our congressman/congresswoman/senator
write to/call the governor/mayor/city manager
speak at a town meeting
send a letter to the newspaper
call a radio talk show

A. You know . . . in my opinion, _____.

B. Why do you say that?

A. _____, _____, and _____.

B. Hmm. You should _____.*

A. _____?

B. Yes. Really. You ought to _____ and express your opinion.

A. That's a good idea. I will.

You're talking with a friend about a local, national, or international issue. Create an original conversation, using the model dialog above as a guide. Feel free to adapt and expand the model any way you wish.

120

Constructions Ahead!

I	
He	
She	
It	} ought to write.
We	
You	
They	

1. My superintendent won't return my security deposit.

   <u>You ought to</u> write a letter to City Hall.

2. Their neighbors leave garbage in the halls!

   _____ call the Health Department.

3. My husband has a fantastic idea!

   _____ express his opinion at the meeting.

4. Anita found pieces of lead paint in her hallway.

   _____ call the Housing Authority.

5. You know . . . we're always on time, we work hard, and we never miss work!

   _____ ask the boss for more money!

Cultural Intersections

In your country, what do citizens do when they are dissatisfied about something and want to express an opinion?

Do they write or call political leaders?

Do they write letters to newspapers?

Do they call radio talk programs?

Tell about forms of citizen participation in your country.

Your Turn

For Writing and Discussion

What issue do you feel strongly about? Write a letter to a political leader of your country and express your views.

121

Reading: *There Ought to Be a Law*

Mr. and Mrs. Fernandez were worried. It was already December, and they still didn't have heat in their apartment. Every time they called the superintendent of the building, Mr. Grant, he promised to turn on the heat, but he never did.

Last Wednesday, Mrs. Fernandez went to Mr. Grant's office during her lunch break. She told him that it was very cold in the apartment and that her children were getting sick. She told him that they always paid* their rent on time and that it was his job to fix the heat in their apartment.

Mr. Grant listened politely to Mrs. Fernandez. He told her that he was very busy and that he had to take care of many things in the building. "You'll have heat very soon," he promised.

Three days passed, but the Fernandez family still didn't have any heat. Mr. Fernandez told his problem to a neighbor. "There ought to be a law," he said. "I think my family should have heat in the winter!" "But there IS a law!" the neighbor said. "Didn't you know that? You should contact the Housing Authority."

A man at the Housing Authority listened to Mr. Fernandez's story. He told Mr. Fernandez that Mr. Grant had to fix the heating system immediately. The man promised to call Mr. Grant and tell him to fix it.

Later that same day, there was heat! Mr. and Mrs. Fernandez couldn't believe it! Mr. Grant came by the apartment to make sure that the system was working well. He apologized and said, "I have a lot of problems in the building and I can't do everything myself. Please be patient the next time you have a problem. And please don't call the Housing Authority!" "Oh," said Mr. Fernandez, "I'm sure that won't be necessary."

What's the Answer?

1 Mr. and Mrs. Fernandez called Mr. Grant _____.
- a. to be polite
- b. because Mr. Grant was very worried
- c. because they needed heat

2 Mr. Grant always promised to _____.
- a. turn on the heat
- b. never turn on the heat
- c. call during December

3 Mrs. Fernandez went to Mr. Grant's office to _____.
- a. pay the rent
- b. repair the heating system
- c. ask for his help

4 Mr. Grant listened to her. Then he _____.
- a. was polite, but didn't help her
- b. was polite, and helped her immediately
- c. was very impolite

5 Three days later, _____.
- a. a neighbor fixed their heat
- b. they had heat in their apartment
- c. Mr. Grant went to the Housing Authority

6 There's a law that _____.
- a. it's cold in the winter
- b. tenants have to have heat during the winter
- c. you have to contact the Housing Authority

*pay–paid

7 The Housing Authority called Mr. Grant _____.

    a. to help him fix the heating system

    b. to tell him to fix the heat

    c. three days later

8 Mr. Grant came by the Fernandez's apartment and _____.

    a. promised to be patient the next time

    b. apologized to the Housing Authority

    c. apologized to Mr. and Mrs. Fernandez

9 Mr. Fernandez said, "I'm sure that won't be necessary." He means he won't have to _____.

    a. fix the heat himself

    b. call the Housing Authority

    c. call Mr. Grant

10 When the Fernandez family has a problem in the future, Mr. Grant will probably _____.

    a. call the Housing Authority

    b. be very patient

    c. help them immediately

InterActions

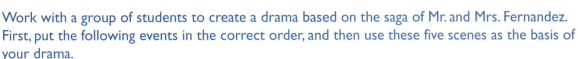

Work with a group of students to create a drama based on the saga of Mr. and Mrs. Fernandez. First, put the following events in the correct order, and then use these five scenes as the basis of your drama.

> _____ Mr. Fernandez goes to the Housing Authority.
>
> _____ Mrs. Fernandez goes to Mr. Grant's office.
>
>   1   Mrs. and Mrs. Fernandez call Mr. Grant about their heating problem.
>
> _____ Mr. Grant visits Mr. and Mrs. Fernandez.
>
> _____ Mr. Fernandez talks to his neighbor.

Compare the different groups' interpretations of the story.

CrossTalk

Talk with a partner about your reactions to Mr. and Mrs. Fernandez's problem.

What is your opinion of Mr. Grant's behavior?

Do you think Mr. and Mrs. Grant did the right thing?

Do you think they'll have more problems with Mr. Grant in the future?

Compare with other students' opinions.

□ **Housing**
apartment
balcony
building
entrance
garbage
hall
heat
kitchen
laundry
lead paint
noise
roof
rules
security deposit
tenant
TV antenna
window ledge

□ **Recreation**
camp
fish
ice skate
play ball
swim

□ **Signs**
Do Not Enter
Keep Off the
  Grass
No Fishing
No Food or
  Drinks
No Parking
No Smoking
No Standing in
  Front of the
  White Line

Parking for
  Handicapped
  Only

□ **Road Signs**
Do Not Enter
No Left Turn
No Right Turn on
  Red
No U Turn
One Way
Stop

□ **Driving**
illegal
license
90 miles per hour
Officer

red light
road
stop sign
ticket
U turn
wrong side of the
  road
drive
drive through *a
  stop sign*
go *90* miles per
  hour
go through *a red
  light*
make *an illegal U
  turn*
speed

□ **Household
  Repairs**
fix *my sink*
remove *the lead
  paint*
repair *our toilet*
spray *our
  apartment*
turn on *our heat*

□ **Tenants' Rights**
Channel 7 News
City Hall
court
Health
  Department
Housing Authority

□ **Citizen
  Participation**
call
express *your
  opinion*
send a letter
speak
write to
city manager
congressman
congresswoman
governor
mayor
president
senator

newspaper
radio talk show
town meeting

Now Leaving Exit 6 Construction Area

□ **Impersonal Expressions with *You***
□ **Past Continuous Tense**
□ **Must**
□ **Ought to**
□ **Should**

Sorry for the inconvenience. For more information see page 175.

ExpressWays Checklist

I can...
□ ask what you're allowed to do
□ tell people what they're allowed to do
□ understand traffic signs
□ understand traffic violations
□ understand rules of an apartment
  building
□ deal effectively with housing
  problems
□ understand rules and regulations at
  work sites
□ express opinions about issues that
  concern me

REST STOP
Take a break!
Have a conversation!

Here are some scenes from Exits 4, 5, and 6.

Who do you think these people are?
What do you think they're talking about?

In pairs or small groups, create conversations based on these scenes and act them out.

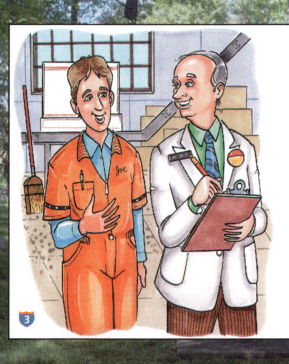

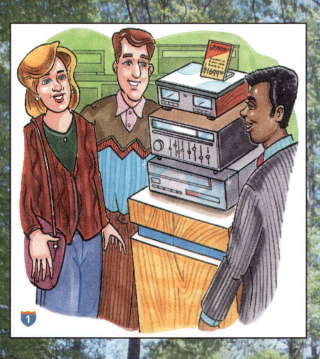

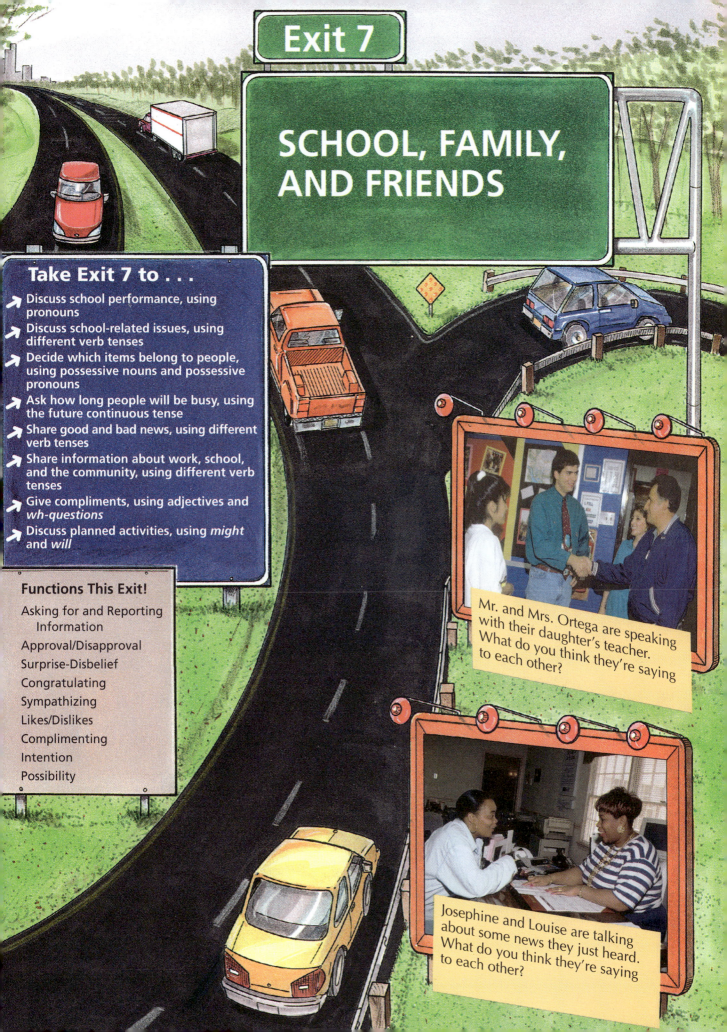

Exit 7

SCHOOL, FAMILY, AND FRIENDS

Take Exit 7 to . . .

- Discuss school performance, using pronouns
- Discuss school-related issues, using different verb tenses
- Decide which items belong to people, using possessive nouns and possessive pronouns
- Ask how long people will be busy, using the future continuous tense
- Share good and bad news, using different verb tenses
- Share information about work, school, and the community, using different verb tenses
- Give compliments, using adjectives and *wh-questions*
- Discuss planned activities, using *might* and *will*

Functions This Exit!

Asking for and Reporting
    Information
Approval/Disapproval
Surprise-Disbelief
Congratulating
Sympathizing
Likes/Dislikes
Complimenting
Intention
Possibility

Mr. and Mrs. Ortega are speaking with their daughter's teacher. What do you think they're saying to each other?

Josephine and Louise are talking about some news they just heard. What do you think they're saying to each other?

A. Hello. I'm Mrs. Carter.

B. Oh! David's mother! I'm pleased to meet you.

A. Nice to meet you, too. Tell me, how is David doing in Math this year?

B. He's doing very well. He works very hard, and his grades are excellent. You should be very proud of him.

A. I'm happy to hear that. Thank you.

1 Mr. Taylor
Judy

2 Mrs. Lee
George

3 Mr. and Mrs. Williams
Beth

4 Mrs. Mitchell
Tommy and Timmy

5 Mr. Atlas
Jack

It's "Open House" at school. Talk with a teacher about your son or daughter.

Fill It In!

Fill in the correct word.

I	you	he	she	we	they
my	your	his	her	our	their
me	you	him	her	us	them

Alan isn't a careful driver. The police always stop _____ him _____[1] and give _____ him _____[2] tickets. The next time _____ he _____[3] gets a ticket, I'm sure the police will take away _____ his _____[4] driver's license.

The sales clerks in the Men's Clothing Department are excellent workers. _____[5] never make mistakes, and _____[6] take inventory very well. Maybe we should give _____[7] raises.

Don't be afraid to express _____[8] opinion! _____[9] can write to _____[10] local newspaper. _____[11] can even send a letter to _____[12] representative in Congress.

Jennifer is seventeen years old. She has a part-time job. _____[13] works very hard, and _____[14] puts a lot of _____[15] salary in the bank. _____[16] is saving money to pay for _____[17] college tuition. _____[18] parents are very proud of _____[19].

I like to study English. _____[20] teacher is very nice. He always understands _____[21] and helps _____[22] with _____[23] homework when _____[24] have trouble with it.

129

My Family's Favorite School Subjects

| Science o | History | Math | Physical Education | French o | Spelling |

Everybody in our family enjoys school at lot! My brother Tom likes to work with numbers. His best class is _____Math_____ 1. My sister Veronica likes sports, so she enjoys _____ 2 the most. My brother Alex loves to study plants, animals, and the weather. He gets excellent grades in _____ 3. My sister Janet likes to study different languages, so her favorite class is _____ 4. I really enjoy learning about the presidents, especially Abraham Lincoln. I do well in _____ 5. And my little sister Angie just started first grade. She doesn't know the alphabet very well, so she's having a lot of trouble with _____ 6.

InterView

Interview ten people and ask them the following questions about school subjects. You can ask students in your class or any other people you know.

What's your favorite subject?
Why is it your favorite?

For you, which subject is the easiest?
Which is the most difficult?
Which is the most interesting?
Which is the most boring?

Which subject do you think most people will say is their favorite? the easiest? the most difficult? the most interesting? the most boring? Make a chart of everyone's responses and tabulate the results. Did you predict the results correctly?

Reading: *Extracurricular Activities*

My friends and I are involved in a lot of extracurricular activites at school.

My friend Greta plays the trombone in the school band.

Peter is in the school orchestra. He plays the violin.

Barbara and Mark sing in the school choir.

My friend Tina acts in all the school plays. Everybody says she's the most talented actress in the drama club.

Many of my friends are good athletes. Mike plays on the football team. Richard plays on the baseball team. And Caroline plays on the school tennis team.

I'm more the "literary type." I write articles for the school newspaper, and I write short stories and poetry for our school literary magazine. In addition, I'm the editor of our yearbook.

And my best friend, Connie, is very active in student government. In fact, she's the president of our senior class.

My friends and I enjoy our school subjects, and we especially enjoy all of the wonderful extracurricular activities we're involved in.

CrossTalk

Talk with a partner about YOUR favorite extracurricular activities at school.

Cultural Intersections

Tell about schools in your country.

What subjects do students usually take?
What are the most popular extracurricular activities?
Is there an "Open House" evening when parents visit the school and talk with their
   children's teachers? Tell about these events.

Report to the class and compare schools in different places.

This Is Mrs. Smith, the School Principal, Calling

A. Hello?

B. Hello. Is this Mr. Johnson?

A. Yes, it is.

B. This is Mrs. Smith, the school principal, calling.

A. Yes?

B. Michael started a fight in the school cafeteria this morning.

A. He did?

B. I'm afraid he did.

A. All right. I promise I'll speak to him about this when he gets home. Thank you for letting me know.

B. You're welcome. Good-bye.

Mr. Johnson

Mrs. Smith, the school principal

1. Mrs. Thomas
Mr. Baker, Wendy's History teacher

2. Mrs. Lane
Miss Fenwick, the school nurse

3. Ms. Wilkins
Mr. Mendoza, Patty's guidance counselor

4. Mr. Robertson
Ms. Pepper, Diane's homeroom teacher

5. Mr. Simmons
Coach Bradley

Someone from school is calling about a problem with your child.

What's the Answer?

1. Excuse me. Is this Room 18?   Yes, _____*it is*_____.
2. Did your son do his homework last night? No, _____.
3. Was the History test very hard?   Yes, _____.
4. Are your daughter's grades good?   Yes, _____.
5. Are you going to cut class today?   No, _____.
6. Did Mr. Grimes, the principal, call your parents? Yes, _____.
7. Do your friends help you with your homework? No, _____.
8. Are you going to be late for school today? Yes, _____.

Who's Talking?

REFLECTIONS
Do any children in your family go to school? What kind of communication do you have with the school? Who do you talk with? Do you have any problems with the school? How can you solve them?

869

Discuss in pairs or small groups, and then share your ideas with the class.

_b_ 1. I'll give you some aspirin.

a. *guidance counselor*

_____ 2. Are there any questions about today's grammar?

b. *school nurse*

_____ 3. Throw the ball!

c. *custodian*

_____ 4. Maria, we need to talk about your plans for college.

d. *principal*

_____ 5. May I interrupt class to fix a light?

e. *coach*

_____ 6. Mrs. Green. We're having some trouble with your son, Jimmy.

f. *English teacher*

75

133

Whose Things Are These?

larger

A. Whose sock is this? Is it yours?

B. No. It isn't mine. I think it's Dad's.

A. Gee, I don't think so. His is larger.

B. I'll ask him.

smaller

A. Whose sneakers are these? Are they yours?

B. No. They aren't mine. I think they're Mom's.

A. Gee, I don't think so. Hers are smaller.

B. I'll ask her.

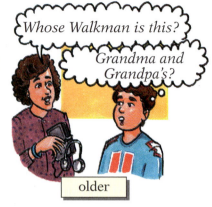

older

A. Whose Walkman is this? Is it yours?

B. No. It isn't mine. I think it's Grandma and Grandpa's.

A. Gee, I don't think so. Theirs is older.

B. I'll ask them.

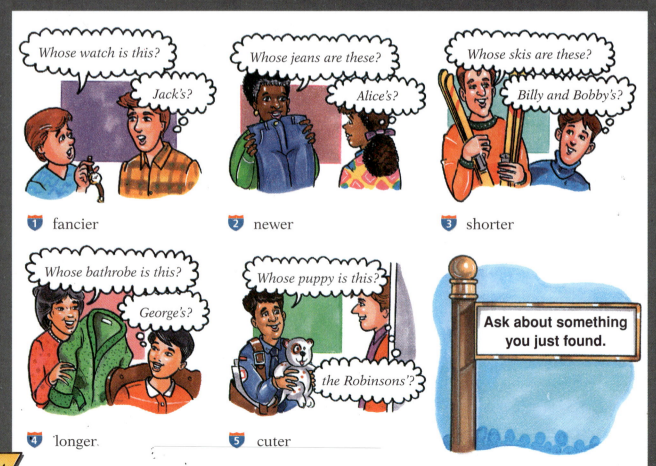

1 fancier

2 newer

3 shorter

4 longer

5 cuter

Ask about something you just found.

Constructions Ahead!

I	mine
he	his
she	hers
we	ours
you	yours
they	theirs

1. This book belongs to me. I'm sure it's ___mine___.

2. I think this is Barbara's coat. Yes, I'm positive it's _____.

3. Tom, I think this is your pen. In fact, I'm sure it's _____.

4. My brother and I both have notebook computers. His computer is more powerful than _____, but my computer is much lighter than _____.

5. My husband and I take a lot of home movies, and our neighbors do, too. Today we're watching _____, and they're watching _____.

Matching Lines

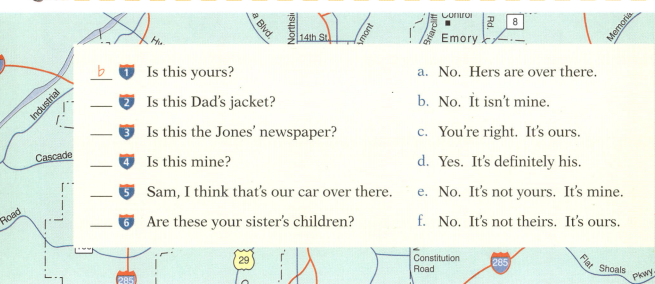

_b_ 1. Is this yours?   a. No. Hers are over there.

___ 2. Is this Dad's jacket?   b. No. It isn't mine.

___ 3. Is this the Jones' newspaper? c. You're right. It's ours.

___ 4. Is this mine?   d. Yes. It's definitely his.

___ 5. Sam, I think that's our car over there. e. No. It's not yours. It's mine.

___ 6. Are these your sister's children? f. No. It's not theirs. It's ours.

How Much Longer?

talk on the phone

A. How much longer will you be talking on the phone?

B. For another half hour.

A. For another half hour?

B. Uh-húh. I'll be talking on the phone for another half hour. Is that okay?

A. I guess so.

1 vacuum the rugs

2 watch this program

3 practice the piano

4 use the bathroom

5 use the hair dryer

Ask how much longer somebody will be doing something.

Constructions Ahead!

(I will)	I'll
(He will)	He'll
(She will)	She'll
(It will)	It'll
(We will)	We'll
(You will)	You'll
(They will)	They'll

} be working.

1 **A.** How much longer will you be studying?

B. ___I'll be studying___ for another hour.

2 **A.** How much longer will Sally be using the shower?

B. _____ the shower for a few more minutes.

3 **A.** How much longer will Paul be working here?

B. _____ here until the end of the month.

4 **A.** How much longer will it be raining?

B. _____ for another two days.

5 **A.** How much longer will I be staying here in the hospital?

B. _____ here for a few more days.

6 **A.** How much longer will we be flying over the airport?

B. _____ over the airport until we have permission to land.

7 **A.** How much longer will those dogs be barking?

B. _____ until their family comes home.

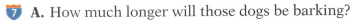

Good News! Bad News!

I just got a raise!

A. What's new with you?
B. Not much. How about you?
A. I have some good news.
B. Really? What is it?
A. I just got a raise!
B. That's great! Congratulations!

My husband got fired last week!

A. What's new with you?
B. Not much. How about you?
A. I have some bad news.
B. Really? What is it?
A. My husband got fired last week!
B. That's too bad. I'm sorry to hear that.

1.  My daughter was just accepted to medical school!

2.  My brother and his wife are getting a divorce!

3.  I won* $10,000 in the lottery!

4.  Our house has termites!

5.  I'm going to have a baby!

Share some good news and some bad news with somebody.

*win—won

Crossed Lines

Put the following lines in the correct order.

_____ I'm going to be transferred to another city, and my family is upset about it.

_____ Let's hear the good news first.

_____ Pretty good. What's new?

_____ Okay. I was just promoted.

_____ That's too bad. I'm sorry to hear that. I hope you can work something out.

_____ Thanks.

_1_ Hi. How are you?

_____ Well, I have some good news and some bad news. Which do you want to hear first?

_____ That's great! Congratulations! And what's the bad news?

Listen

Listen and choose the best response.

1️⃣ a. Congratulations!
   b. That's too bad.

2️⃣ a. I'm sorry to hear that.
   b. That's great!

3️⃣ a. That's great!
   b. That's too bad!

4️⃣ a. Congratulations!
   b. Sorry to hear that.

5️⃣ a. Sorry to hear that.
   b. That's great!

6️⃣ a. That's too bad!
   b. Congratulations!

Your Turn

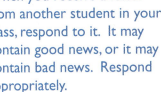

For Writing and Discussion

Write a letter to a classmate in which you tell about something that recently happened to you. It may be good news, or it may be bad news.

When you receive a letter from another student in your class, respond to it. It may contain good news, or it may contain bad news. Respond appropriately.

139

A. Did you hear the news?
B. No. What?
A. The city bus drivers are going on strike!
B. Really? Where did you hear that?
A. I read it in the paper.

1 I heard it on the radio.

2 I overheard it in the cafeteria.

3 Someone in Science class told* me.

4 The whole school is talking about it.

5 The neighbors are whispering about it.

Tell about some news you just heard!

*tell-told
break-broke

Listen

Listen and put the number under the correct picture.

_____ _____ _____

_____ 1 _____

_____ _____ _____

CrossTalk

Do you know any rumors? Do you think they're true? Whisper the rumors to a partner and then tell the class.

Community Connections

Look in your local newspaper for a piece of news you think is interesting or important. Cut out the article and bring it to class. Talk with a partner about the following:

Who are the people mentioned?

What happened?

When did it take place?

Where did it happen?

Why is the article interesting or important?

141

A. I really like your new laptop computer. It's very light!
B. Thanks.
A. How much does it weigh?
B. It weighs about two pounds.

1. car
   smooth

2. rug
   colorful

3. haircut
   flattering

4. kitten
   cute

5. motorcycle
   powerful

Compliment somebody on something!

Fill It In!

Fill in the correct word.

1 Your new car is very ____!
  a. flattering
  (b.) powerful

2 I like my new tennis racket because it's very ____.
  a. light
  b. right

3 Your new sports jacket is extremely ____.
  a. intelligent
  b. colorful

4 When I use Soapy Shave Creme, my face feels very ____.
  a. smooth
  b. cute

5 This new motorcycle is extremely ____.
  a. powerful
  b. flattering

6 What a ____ little puppy!
  a. big
  b. cute

What's the Question?

1 What _____did you see_____ ? — We saw *Star Battles*.

2 Why _____ ? — I'm leaving because it's late.

3 Where _____ ? — I got it at Ace Appliances.

4 How _____ ? — I feel much better, thanks.

5 When _____ ? — You'll get a raise in a few months.

6 What _____ ? — Nothing happened.

7 Who _____ ? — My neighbor told me.

8 Why _____ ? — I stopped because I don't need any more practice.

CrossTalk

Talk with a partner about giving and accepting compliments.

I really like that tie!

How do you feel when someone compliments you?
What do you say?
Do you compliment other people often?
What do you compliment them about?

INTERCHANGE

What Are You Going to Do This Weekend?

What are you going to do this weekend?

A. What are you going to do this weekend?

B. I'm not sure. I'll probably stay home and study English. How about you?

A. I don't know. I might go to a museum, or I might spend some time with my grandparents. I'm not sure yet.

B. Well, whatever you decide to do, I hope you enjoy yourself.

A. Thanks. You, too.

A. What are you going to do _____?

B. I'm not sure. I'll probably _____. How about you?

A. I don't know. I might _____, or I might

_____. I'm not sure yet.

B. Well, whatever you decide to do, I hope you enjoy yourself.

A. Thanks. You, too.

What are you going to do on your next day off?

What are you going to do on your next vacation?

What are you going to do over the holiday?

You and an acquaintance are talking about your plans. Create an original conversation, using the model dialog above as a guide. Feel free to adapt and expand the model any way you wish.

Constructions Ahead!

| I |
| He |
| She |
| It | } might leave. |
| We |
| You |
| They |

1 What are you going to do this vacation?

I don't know. _____ I might _____ drive to the mountains.

2 What's the weather forecast for the weekend?

I'm not sure. _____ rain, or _____ be nice.

3 What are you and your wife going to do when you retire?

We aren't sure. _____ move to Arizona.

4 What's your son going to do when he finishes college?

He doesn't know. _____ go to business school.

5 What's your wife going to do for your 50th birthday?

I don't know. _____ give me a surprise party.

6 I'm a very nervous person. What can I do to relax?

_____ try meditation.

7 What's your family going to say when you tell them you're going skydiving?

I'm not sure. _____ tell me I'm crazy!

Your Turn

For Writing and Discussion

Describe an ideal vacation or an ideal day off from work.

On your ideal vacation or day off, what will you do?
Where will you go?
How will you feel?

Share your plans with other students and see how their plans compare with yours.

REFLECTIONS
What do people do during the weekend and on vacations in different countries you know? Are the activities the same or different?

Discuss in pairs or small groups, and then share your ideas with the class.

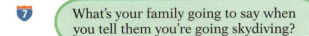

Looking Back

☐ **School Subjects**
French
History
Math
Physical Education
 (gym class)
Science
Spelling

☐ **School Personnel**
advisor
coach

guidance
 counselor
homeroom teacher
nurse
principal
teacher

☐ **Extracurricular Activities**
band
baseball team
choir
drama club

football team
literary magazine
newspaper
orchestra
student
 government
tennis team
yearbook

☐ **Additional School Vocabulary**
cafeteria

class
eye test
grades
homework
senior class picnic

☐ **Employment Vocabulary**
get fired
go on strike
raise

☐ **Describing**
colorful
cute
flattering
light
powerful
smooth

Now Leaving Exit 7 Construction Area

☐ **Possessive Nouns**
☐ **Possessive Pronouns**
☐ **Pronoun Review**
☐ **Short Answers**
☐ **Future Continuous Tense**
☐ **Time Expressions**
☐ **WH-Questions**
☐ **Tense Review**
☐ **Might**

Sorry for the inconvenience. For more information see pages 176 and 177.

ExpressWays Checklist

I can...
☐ discuss school performance
☐ discuss school-related issues
☐ decide which items belong to different people
☐ ask how long people will be busy
☐ share good and bad news about friends and family members
☐ share information about work, school, and the community
☐ give compliments
☐ discuss planned activities

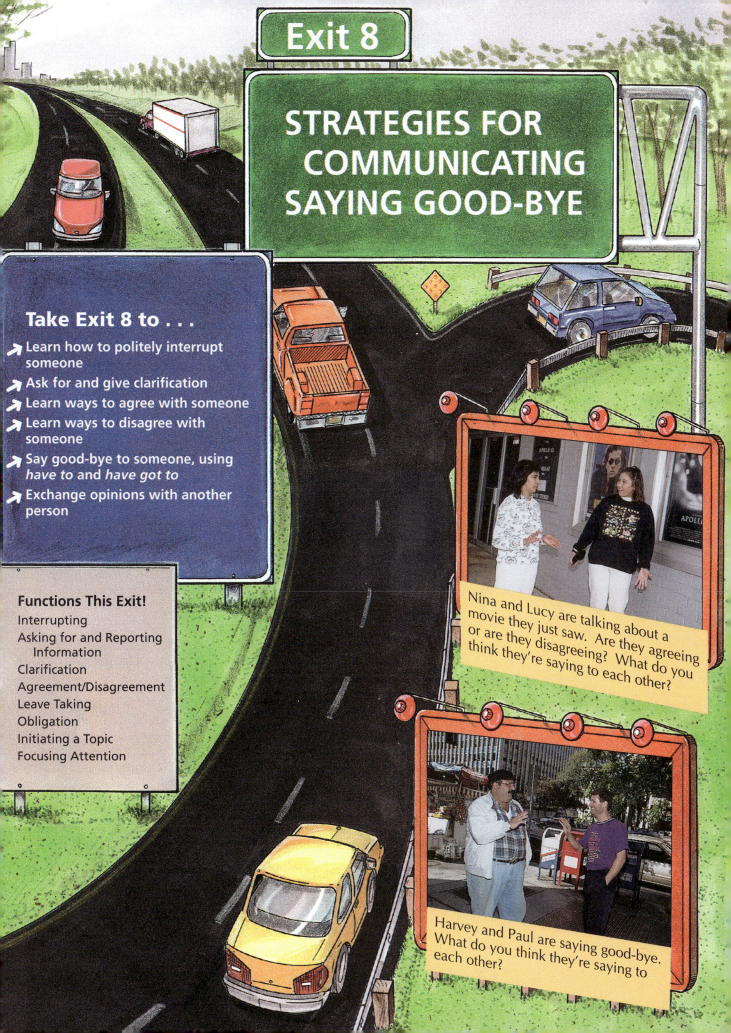

Exit 8

STRATEGIES FOR COMMUNICATING SAYING GOOD-BYE

Take Exit 8 to . . .

- Learn how to politely interrupt someone
- Ask for and give clarification
- Learn ways to agree with someone
- Learn ways to disagree with someone
- Say good-bye to someone, using *have to* and *have got to*
- Exchange opinions with another person

Functions This Exit!

Interrupting
Asking for and Reporting
    Information
Clarification
Agreement/Disagreement
Leave Taking
Obligation
Initiating a Topic
Focusing Attention

Nina and Lucy are talking about a movie they just saw. Are they agreeing or are they disagreeing? What do you think they're saying to each other?

Harvey and Paul are saying good-bye. What do you think they're saying to each other?

A. Excuse me. I'm sorry to interrupt, but we're out of fries.
B. Did you say pies?
A. No. Fries.
B. Oh, okay. Thank you.

Crossed Lines

Put the following lines in the correct order.

_____ Did you say her NOSE?

__1__ Excuse me, Doctor. I'm sorry to interrupt, . . .

_____ Oh. I'll go to her room right away.

_____ but there's a problem with Mrs. Miller's toes.

_____ No. There's a problem with her TOES!

Matching Lines

Match and pronounce.

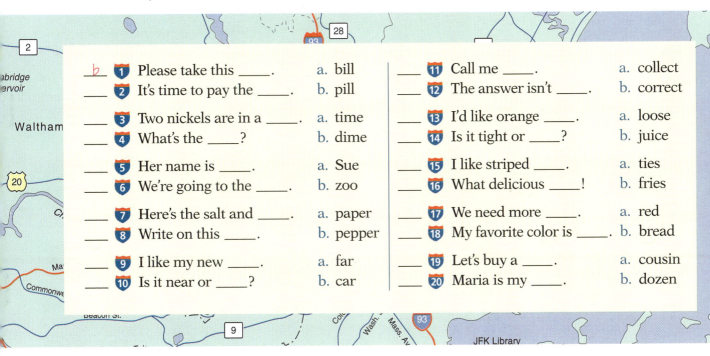

__b__ **1** Please take this _____.   a. bill
___ **2** It's time to pay the _____.   b. pill

___ **3** Two nickels are in a _____.   a. time
___ **4** What's the _____?   b. dime

___ **5** Her name is _____.   a. Sue
___ **6** We're going to the _____.   b. zoo

___ **7** Here's the salt and _____.   a. paper
___ **8** Write on this _____.   b. pepper

___ **9** I like my new _____.   a. far
___ **10** Is it near or _____?   b. car

___ **11** Call me _____.   a. collect
___ **12** The answer isn't _____.   b. correct

___ **13** I'd like orange _____.   a. loose
___ **14** Is it tight or _____?   b. juice

___ **15** I like striped _____.   a. ties
___ **16** What delicious _____!   b. fries

___ **17** We need more _____.   a. red
___ **18** My favorite color is _____.   b. bread

___ **19** Let's buy a _____.   a. cousin
___ **20** Maria is my _____.   b. dozen

Listen

Listen and choose the word you hear.

1 (a.) Hale   **3** a. mother   **5** a. noise   **7** a. elevator
　　 b. Dale   b. brother   b. boys   b. escalator

2 a. Monday   **4** a. rice   **6** a. eat   **8** a. chicken
　　 b. Sunday   b. ice   b. heat   b. kitchen

CrossTalk

In your opinion, when is it appropriate to interrupt someone who is speaking? Talk with a partner. (Try not to interrupt each other!) Then report to the class and compare ideas.

What Does That Mean?

"They aren't working right now."

A. Our computers are down.

B. I'm afraid I'm not following you. What does that mean?

A. That means they aren't working right now.

B. Oh. I understand.

1 "There aren't any more seats on the plane."

2 "You're in excellent health."

3 "I'll pay for the dinner."

4 "He quit.*"

5 "It's very popular."

Ask someone to clarify something.

*throw—threw
quit—quit

What Does It Mean?

Choose the correct meaning.

Everybody says this movie is really hot in New York!

1 a. The movie theaters in New York don't have air conditioning.
   b. A lot of New Yorkers are going to see the movie.

Sorry. The flight is overbooked.

2 a. They're going to have to find another flight.
   b. These people took too many books and newspapers on the airplane.

According to my doctor, the tests were negative!

3 a. This patient doesn't have to worry.
   b. The results of the test were very bad.

Timothy, this will be my treat!

4 a. They'll eat delicious food.
   b. She'll pay the check.

Matching Lines

What do you think the following expressions mean?

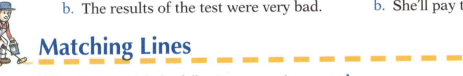

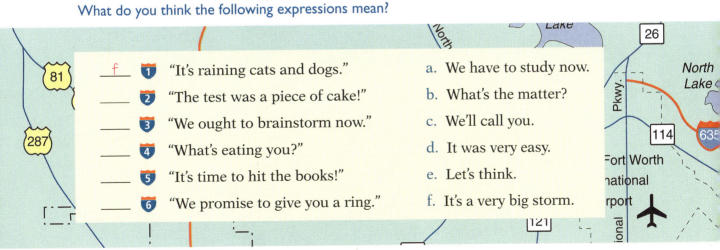

_f_ **1** "It's raining cats and dogs."	a. We have to study now.
____ **2** "The test was a piece of cake!"	b. What's the matter?
____ **3** "We ought to brainstorm now."	c. We'll call you.
____ **4** "What's eating you?"	d. It was very easy.
____ **5** "It's time to hit the books!"	e. Let's think.
____ **6** "We promise to give you a ring."	f. It's a very big storm.

Cultural Intersections

In your country, is it common for people to treat others in restaurants? What is your opinion of this custom?

A. You know . . . the boss is in a terrible mood today.

B. I agree. He is.

A. We probably shouldn't bother him.

B. You're right. I was thinking the same thing.

ExpressWays

1 Sally's grandfather is very interesting!

I agree. _____He is_____.

2 I love my family.

I know. _____.

3 This food looks delicious!

You're right. _____.

4 This is a very long report!

I agree. _____.

5 These pain pills are powerful!

I know. _____.

6 Your brother takes too many vitamins!

You're right. _____.

7 Aunt Rose made fantastic spaghetti!

I agree. _____.

8 Alice will find a job soon.

I know. _____.

9 That movie wasn't very funny!

You're right. _____.

10 The expressway was very crowded today.

I agree. _____.

Listen

Listen and choose the correct response.

1 a. He is?
(b.) He was?

2 a. It won't?
b. It did?

3 a. They do?
b. They are?

4 a. We do?
b. We have?

5 a. She has?
b. She does?

6 a. He did?
b. They did?

7 a. It does?
b. It is?

8 a. He wasn't?
b. He isn't?

9 a. She is?
b. She did?

CrossTalk

Talk with a partner and find five things about your English class that you agree about. Tell your agreements to the class and see if others also agree with you.

A. You know . . . I think this bread is stale.

B. Oh? Why do you say that?

A. It feels very hard. Don't you agree?

B. No, not really. I disagree.

Fill It In!

Complete the following conversations by filling in the correct last line.

> a. She looks really relaxed.
> b. She's wearing a new ring.
> c. She was late again today.
> d. She's a very efficient worker.

1 **A.** You know . . . I'm afraid Barbara will get fired.

B. Oh? Why do you say that?

A. ___c___

2 **A.** You know . . . I think Sally had a fantastic vacation.

B. Oh? Why do you say that?

A. ____

3 **A.** You know . . . I think our English teacher is going to get married soon.

B. Oh? Why do you say that?

A. ____

4 **A.** You know . . . I think Carmen is going to be promoted soon.

B. Oh? Why do you say that?

A. ____

Listen

Listen and decide where each conversation is taking place.

1 a. in a bank
   b. in a doctor's office

2 a. in a dentist's office
   b. in a drug store

3 a. in an elevator
   b. on an expressway

4 a. in an employee lounge
   b. in a laundromat

5 a. in a department store
   b. in a theater

6 a. in a dressing room
   b. in an elevator

7 a. in a library
   b. in a hotel

8 a. in a clinic
   b. in someone's kitchen

9 a. in a pharmacy
   b. in a restaurant

InterView

Make a list of ten opinions you have. Interview students in the class and other people you know. See who agrees with you and who disagrees with you.

get back to work

A. By the way, what time is it?

B. It's 1:30.

A. Oh! It's late! I've really got to go now. I have to get back to work.

B. Okay. See you soon.

A. Good-bye.

1 pick up my kids at school

2 get to class

3 mail these letters before the post office closes

4 get to the bank by 4:00

5 be at the White House in ten minutes

It's late! You've got to go now.

Constructions Ahead!

I've We've You've They've }	got to	=	I We You They }	have to	
					work.
He's She's It's }	got to	=	He She It }	has to	

1 Jane has a lot of homework. <u>She's got to</u> finish it before she goes to bed.

2 My wife and I are late for a meeting. Sorry. _____ leave right now.

3 Your husband is having some medical problems? _____ see a doctor right away!

4 Mr. and Mrs. Martini are in a hurry. _____ get to the post office before it closes.

5 You're late! _____ leave right now!

It's almost midnight?! _____ go now.
Good-bye.

6

Fill It In!

Fill in the correct word.

1 I should be home ____ half an hour.
   a. in
   b. by

2 Takashi will get here ____ Maria does.
   a. by
   b. before

3 Natasha will be there ____ 6:30.
   a. in
   b. by

4 Let's go ____ the museum closes.
   a. by
   b. before

5 The guests will be arriving ____ a few minutes.
   a. in
   b. by

6 Tom will be promoted ____ next May.
   a. by
   b. in

7 I can get there ____ five minutes.
   a. in
   b. by

8 Susan knew the answer ____ I did.
   a. in
   b. before

9 I'll call back ____ one hour.
   a. by
   b. in

10 Mr. Peters, please don't leave work ____ 4:00 P.M.
   a. in
   b. before

pick up my wife at the office

A. You know, I think I should be going now. I've got to pick up my wife at the office.

B. I should be going, too.

A. So long.

B. See you soon.

1 be home before dark

2 buy some food for dinner

3 catch the 6:23 train

4 meet with my advisor in five minutes

5 get to my next performance

You and a friend both have to get going. Say good-bye to each other.

Fill It In!

Fill in the correct word.

easy   soon   long   good-bye   going   care   too   hang up

1 So _long_ .

See you _____ .

2 I should be _____ .

Okay. Take _____ .

3 Take it _____ .

You, _____ .

4 I've got to _____ now.

Okay. _____ .

InterActions

This person wants to hang up because somebody is at the door. Do you think this is a good excuse?

A. Oh! Sorry. I've got to hang up now.
Somebody's at the door.

B. Okay. I'll talk to you soon.

A. All right. Good-bye.

B. Bye.

In your opinion, what are some good excuses for saying good-bye to someone you're speaking to? Talk with a partner and then create conversations using those excuses. Present your conversations to the class and ask other students' opinions of your excuses.

Cultural Intersections

 *So long.*   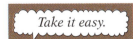 *Take it easy.*    *Bye.*    *Good-bye.*

 *Take care.*    *See you soon.*    *I'll call you soon.*    *Bye-bye.*

There are many different ways of saying "good-bye" in English. Are there also several ways of saying good-bye in your language? What are some of them? Do they have different meanings? When do you use them?

159

INTERCHANGE

In My Opinion

> English is an easy language to learn.

> English is a very difficult language.

> The grammar rules are very easy.

> You don't always pronounce English words the way you spell them.

A. You know . . . I think English is an easy language to learn. Don't you agree?

B. Well, I'm not so sure. Why do you say that?

A. The grammar rules are very easy. Don't you think so?

B. No, not really. I disagree. In my opinion, English is a very difficult language.

A. Oh? What makes you say that?

B. You don't always pronounce English words the way you spell them.

A. Hmm. Maybe you're right.

A. You know . . . I think _____.
Don't you agree?

B. Well, I'm not so sure. Why do you say that?

A. _____. Don't you think so?

B. No, not really. I disagree. In my opinion, _____
_____.

A. Oh? What makes you say that?

B. _____.

A. Hmm. Maybe you're right.

You're having a disagreement with somebody. Create an original conversation, using the model dialog on p. 160 as a guide. Feel free to adapt and expand the model any way you wish.

"How are you?" is a nice question. It's a friendly way that people in the United States greet each other. But "How are you?" is also a very unusual question. It's a question that often doesn't have an answer.

When a person meets a friend on the street and asks "How are you?" the person doesn't really expect to hear an answer such as "I really don't know what's wrong with me. I thought I had an allergy. I took some medicine, but that didn't help much, so I have a doctor's appointment." The person who asks "How are you?" expects to hear the answer "Fine," even if the other person isn't! The reason is that "How are you?" isn't really a question, and "Fine" isn't really an answer. They are simply ways of greeting people and saying "Hello."

Sometimes, people also don't say exactly what they mean. For example, when someone asks "Do you agree?," the other person might be thinking "No, I disagree. I think you're wrong." But it isn't very polite to disagree so strongly, so the other person might say, "I'm not so sure." It's a nicer way to say that you don't agree with someone.

People also don't say exactly what they are thinking when they finish conversations with other people. For example, many conversations over the phone end when one person says, "I've got to go now." Often, the person who wants to hang up gives an excuse: "Someone's at the door." "I've got to put the groceries away." "Something is burning on the stove!" The excuse might be real, or it might not be. Perhaps the person who wants to hang up simply doesn't want to talk any more, but it isn't very polite to say that. The excuse is more polite, and it doesn't hurt the other person's feelings.

Whether they are greeting each other, talking about an opinion, or ending a conversation, people often don't say exactly what they are thinking. It's an important way that people try to be nice to each other, and it's all part of the game of language!

True or False?

1. "How are you?" is a question people use to begin a conversation.

2. "How are you?" is another way of saying "Good-bye."

3. When you ask "How are you?" you don't expect to hear about the other person's health.

4. It's polite to disagree with another person.

5. "I'm not so sure" is a polite way to say you disagree.

6. It's polite to say "I don't want to talk to you any more."

7. According to the reading, all telephone conversations end when one person says, "I've got to go now."

What's the Answer?

1. When a person in the United States asks, "How are you?" he or she expects to hear _____.
   a. "Fine."
   b. "Hello."
   c. "I don't know."

2. When a person wants to disagree with somebody, it is very polite to say _____.
   a. "You're wrong. I disagree."
   b. "I'm not so sure I agree."
   c. "I'm sure I disagree."

3. A polite way to end a conversation is to say _____.
   a. "You have to go now."
   b. "I want to hang up."
   c. "I have to go now."

4. When a person says "I've got to go now. Someone is at the door," the person may be _____.
   a. giving an excuse
   b. hurting someone's feelings
   c. talking to a person at the door

5. One of the rules of the game of language is probably _____.
   a. "Always say what you mean."
   b. "Don't disagree with people."
   c. "Be polite."

Listen

Do the speakers agree or disagree?

1. a. agree
   b. disagree

2. a. agree
   b. disagree

3. a. agree
   b. disagree

4. a. agree
   b. disagree

5. a. agree
   b. disagree

6. a. agree
   b. disagree

7. a. agree
   b. disagree

8. a. agree
   b. disagree

9. a. agree
   b. disagree

Cultural Intersections

In your language, what do people say when they greet each other? How do people disagree politely with each other? What are some ways that people end conversations?

Tell about any "games" in your language.

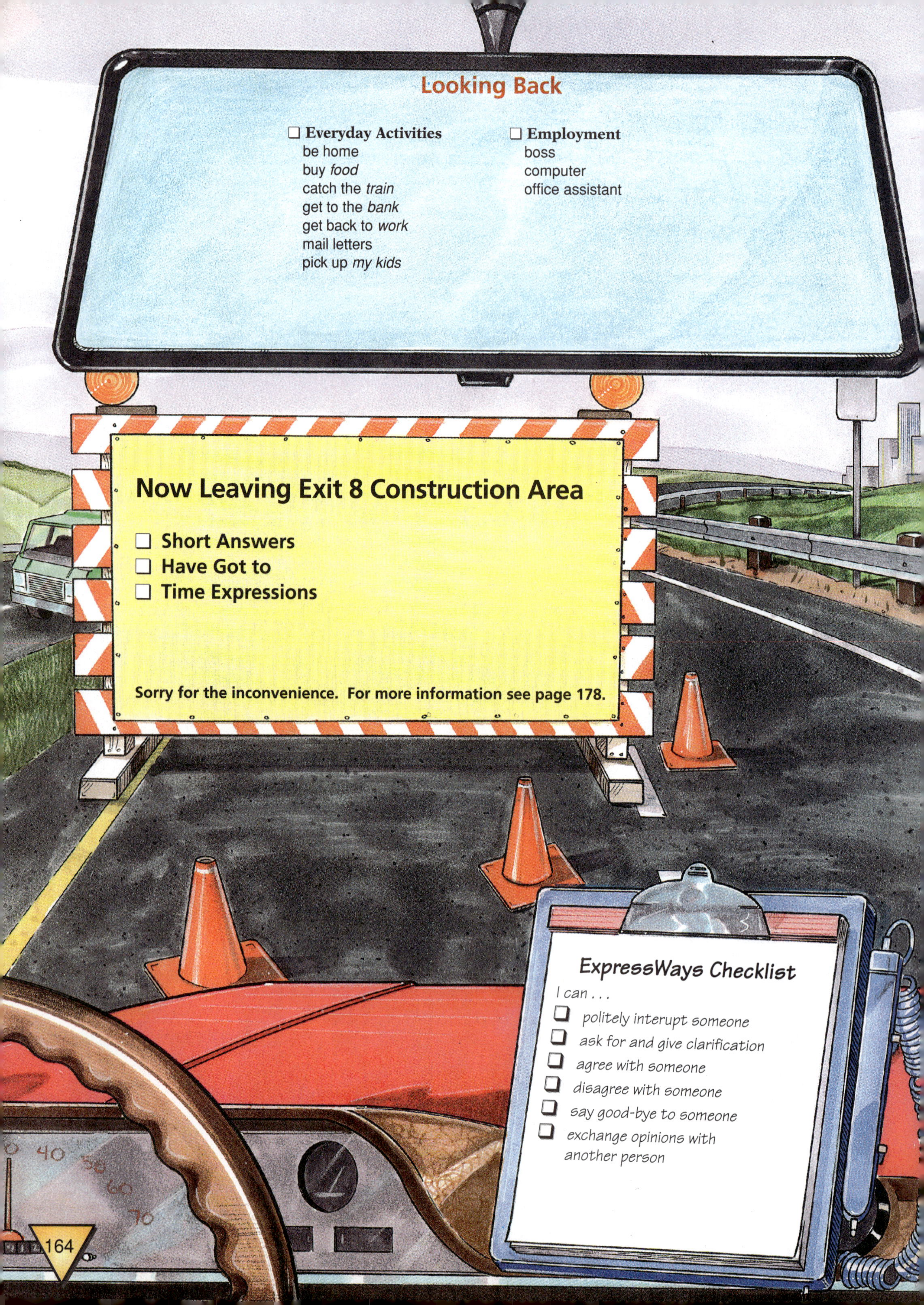

Looking Back

☐ **Everyday Activities**
be home
buy *food*
catch the *train*
get to the *bank*
get back to *work*
mail letters
pick up *my kids*

☐ **Employment**
boss
computer
office assistant

Now Leaving Exit 8 Construction Area

☐ **Short Answers**
☐ **Have Got to**
☐ **Time Expressions**

Sorry for the inconvenience. For more information see page 178.

ExpressWays Checklist

I can . . .

☐ politely interupt someone
☐ ask for and give clarification
☐ agree with someone
☐ disagree with someone
☐ say good-bye to someone
☐ exchange opinions with another person

REST STOP
Take a break!
Have a conversation!

Here are some scenes from Exits 7 and 8.

Who do you think these people are?
What do you think they're talking about?

In pairs or small groups, create conversations based on these scenes and act them out.

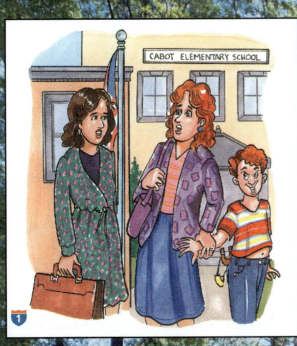

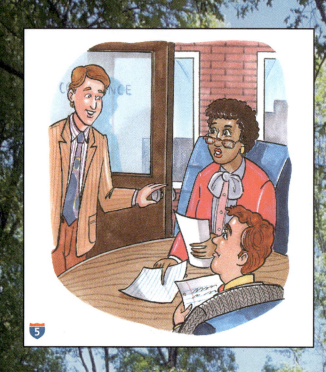

5

6

7

8

166

Appendix

- **Grammar Constructions**
- **Cardinal Numbers**
- **Ordinal Numbers**
- **Irregular Verbs**
- **Scripts for Listening Exercises**
- **Grammar Index**
- **Topic Index**

Exit 1 Constructions

To Be: Present Tense

I	am	
He She It	is	from Mexico.
We You They	are	

Simple Past Tense

I He She It We You They	visited.

To Be: Past Tense

I He She It	was/ wasn't	home.
We You They	were/ weren't	

Simple Present Tense

I We You They	live	in Chicago.
He She It	lives	

Object Pronouns

help	me him her us you them	start the car

Yes/No Questions

Is there a laundromat in the neighborhood?
Are you going to the laundromat?

Do they pick up the garbage today?
Does the mail come on Saturdays?

WH-Questions

What's your major?
Where are you from?
Why are you here?
Which apartment do you live in?

Can

Can I park my car here?
Yes, you **can**.
No, you **can't**.

Should

Maybe you **should** call a plumber.

Two-Word Verbs

clean up	–	**clean** it **up**
cut down	–	**cut** it **down**
hang up	–	**hang** it **up**
pick up	–	**pick** it **up**
put away	–	**put** it **away**
take out	–	**take** it **out**

Time Expressions

I knocked on your door **last week.**
We can send a plumber **at two o'clock this afternoon.**

Exit 2 Constructions

Imperatives

Dial "one."
Dial the area code.
Then, dial the local phone number.

Please fasten your seat belt!
Please don't smoke on the bus!

Prepositions of Location

Please don't lean **against** the doors!
At the corner of Broadway and K Street.
Please stand **behind** the white line!
Please don't ride **between** the cars!
In the parking lot.
In front of the Hilton Hotel.
Near the statue.
On Washington Street.
Please put your bag **under** the seat!

Future: Will

(I will)	I'll	
(He will)	He'll	
(She will)	She'll	
(It will)	It'll	be back soon.
(We will)	We'll	
(You will)	You'll	
(They will)	They'll	

Time Expressions

She'll be back
   in an hour.
   in a few hours.
   in two or three hours.
   in about an hour.
   in a little while.

It's **at** 4:10.

Future: Won't

I		
He		
She		
It	won't	be here until 3:00.
We		
You		
They		

Exit 3 Constructions

Partitives

a bag of potato chips
a bottle of ketchup
a box of rice
a bunch of bananas
a can of tuna fish
a container of cole slaw
a cup of coffee
a dozen eggs
a gallon of orange juice
a glass of milk
a head of lettuce
a jar of mayonnaise
a loaf of bread
an order of french fries
a piece of chicken
a pint of ice cream
a pound of apples
a quart of milk

half a dozen eggs
half a gallon of apple juice
half a pound of cheese

a cup of flour
a tablespoon of water
a teaspoon of salt

Would

What **would** you like?
Would you prefer rice or a
baked potato?

I**'d** like the chicken.
I**'d** prefer a baked potato.

Count/Non-Count Nouns

Count

Would you like **a few** more
meatballs?
Have **a few** more.

They're delicious.
Not **too many**.

Non-Count

Would you like **a little**
more salad?
Have **a little** more.

It's very good.
Not **too much**.

Imperatives

Add half a cup of sugar.
Mix together a cup of flour,
a teaspoon of salt, and
two tablespoons of water.
Put the mixture into a
baking pan.
Bake for one hour.

May

May I help you?

Exit 4 Constructions

Adjectives

It's attractive.
    big.
    comfortable.
    expensive.
    firm.
    good.
    large.
    lightweight.
    nice.
    powerful.
    quiet.

Comparatives

quiet – quieter
large – larger
big – bigger
pretty – prettier

comfortable – more comfortable
attractive – more attractive
powerful – more powerful
expensive – more expensive

good – better

Future: Going to

I'm He's She's It's We're You're They're	going to visit.

Superlatives

firm – the firmest
large – the largest
big – the biggest

lightweight – the most lightweight
powerful – the most powerful

good – the best

Have to

I We You They	have to	work.
He She It	has to	

Should

I He She It We You They	should stop.

Exit 5 Constructions

Adverbs

accurate – accurately
graceful – gracefully
careful – carefully
neat – neatly

good – well
fast – fast

Comparative of Adverbs

fast – faster
loud(ly) – louder
quickly – quicker
slowly – slower

carefully – more carefully
politely – more politely

well – better

Indirect Objects

Please **give** this report **to Mr. Lewis.**
I'll **give him** the report right away.

Reflexive Pronouns

I		myself.
You		yourself.
He		himself.
She	hurt	herself.
It		itself.
We		ourselves.
You		yourselves.
They		themselves.

Two-Word Verbs

clean up the supply room – **clean** it **up**
give out the reports – **give** them **out**
hang up these signs – **hang** them **up**
put away the dishes – **put** them **away**
set up the conference room – **set** it **up**
take down the decorations – **take** them **down**

Could	
I He She It We You They	could/couldn't work.

Able to: Future		
I He She It We You They	will/won't be able to	work.

Able to: Past		
I He She It	was/wasn't able to	work.
We You They	were/weren't able to	

Exit 6 Constructions

Impersonal Expressions with *You*

Are **you** allowed to swim here?
    Yes, **you** are.
    No, **you** aren't.

You aren't allowed to park here.
I don't think **you're** allowed to hang
    your clothes there.

Past Continuous Tense

I He She I	was	driving.
We You They	were	

Must

I He She It We You They	must/mustn't work.

Ought to

I He She It We You They	ought to write.

Should

They **should** have more buses on this route.
You **should** write to the mayor.

Exit 7 Constructions

Possessive Nouns

[s] Jack**'s** father
[z] David**'s** mother
[ɪz] George**'s** mother

Short Answers

I'm afraid | he did.
he didn't.
she is.
she isn't.
he won't.

Pronouns

Subject Pronouns	Object Pronouns	Possessive Adjectives	Possessive Pronouns
I	me	my	mine
He	him	his	his
She	her	her	hers
It	it	its	——
We	us	our	ours
You	you	your	yours
They	them	their	theirs

Future Continuous Tense

(I will)	I'll	
(You will)	You'll	
(He will)	He'll	
(It will)	It'll	be working.
(We will)	We'll	
(You will)	You'll	
(They will)	They'll	

WH-Questions

Who cut it?
What did you name it?
When did you buy it?
Where did you get it?
Why did you buy one?
Whose sock is this?
How much does it weigh?

Time Expressions

| I'll be talking | for | another half hour.
about 10 more minutes.
a few more minutes. |
| | until | 9:00.
the school bus comes. |

Might

| I
He
She
It
We
You
They | might leave. |

Tense Review

He **works** very hard.
Michael **started** a fight.
I'll speak to him.
My brother and his wife **are getting** a divorce.
I'm going to have a baby.

Exit 8 Constructions

Have Got to

I've We've You've They've	got to	=	I We You They	have to	work.
He's She's It's			He She It	has to	

Short Answers

He is
It is.
It isn't.
It does.
He did.
They don't.

Time Expressions

It's **3:00 (three o'clock)**.
It's **1:30 (one thirty)**.
It's **11:20 (eleven twenty)**.
It's **4:45 (four forty-five)**.

I have to mail these letters
   before the post office closes.
   by 4:00.
   in ten minutes.

CARDINAL NUMBERS

1	one	20	twenty
2	two	21	twenty-one
3	three	22	twenty-two
4	four		.
5	five		.
6	six	29	twenty-nine
7	seven	30	thirty
8	eight	40	forty
9	nine	50	fifty
10	ten	60	sixty
11	eleven	70	seventy
12	twelve	80	eighty
13	thirteen	90	ninety
14	fourteen	100	one hundred
15	fifteen	200	two hundred
16	sixteen	300	three hundred
17	seventeen		.
18	eighteen		.
19	nineteen	900	nine hundred
		1,000	one thousand
		2,000	two thousand
		3,000	three thousand
			.
			.
		10,000	ten thousand
		100,000	one hundred thousand
		1,000,000	one million

ORDINAL NUMBERS

1st	first	20th	twentieth
2nd	second	21st	twenty-first
3rd	third	22nd	twenty-second
4th	fourth	.	
5th	fifth	.	
6th	sixth	29th	twenty-ninth
7th	seventh	30th	thirtieth
8th	eighth	40th	fortieth
9th	ninth	50th	fiftieth
10th	tenth	60th	sixtieth
11th	eleventh	70th	seventieth
12th	twelfth	80th	eightieth
13th	thirteenth	90th	ninetieth
14th	fourteenth	100th	one hundredth
15th	fifteenth		
16th	sixteenth	1,000th	one thousandth
17th	seventeenth	1,000,000th	one millionth
18th	eighteenth		
19th	nineteenth		

IRREGULAR VERBS

be	was/were	make	made
bleed	bled	mean	meant
break	broke	meet	met
buy	bought	overhear	overheard
catch	caught	put	put
come	came	quit	quit
cut	cut	read	read
do	did	ride	rode
drive	drove	ring	rang
eat	ate	run	ran
fall	fell	say	said
feed	fed	see	saw
feel	felt	send	sent
find	found	set	set
fit	fit	sit	sat
forget	forgot	speak	spoke
get	got	spend	spent
give	gave	stand	stood
go	went	steal	stole
hang	hung	sweep	swept
have	had	swim	swam
hear	heard	take	took
hit	hit	teach	taught
hold	held	tell	told
hurt	hurt	think	thought
keep	kept	throw	threw
know	knew	understand	understood
lay	laid	wake	woke
leave	left	wear	wore
lend	lent	win	won
lie	lay	write	wrote
lose	lost		

Page 5

Listen and choose the correct answer.

1. Can I ask you a question?
2. Where do you live?
3. Do they deliver mail today?
4. Where does your next-door neighbor work?
5. When do they open the laundromat?
6. Does the superintendent live on the first floor?
7. Is there a school nearby?
8. How many apartments are there in the building?
9. What time do they pick up the garbage?

Page 15

Listen and write the number next to the correct picture.

1. You should call an electrician.
2. Shirley is trying to fix the bathroom sink.
3. The mechanic is going to fix it right now.
4. It's leaking all over the floor!
5. You should call the gas company.
6. We called a carpenter.

Page 17

Listen and choose the correct response.

1. Do you fix light switches?
2. What's the trouble?
3. I can send an electrician tomorrow afternoon. Okay?
4. What's the name?
5. And the address?
6. And the phone number?

Page 27

Listen and choose the word you hear.

1. My friend's name is Ellen.
2. Could I please speak to Nickie?
3. I'm calling Mr. Dannon.

4. Their teacher's name is Mrs. Pratt.
5. The area code is four-one-five.
6. The park closes at eleven.
7. I have an interview with Mr. Zales at three o'clock.
8. Please see Mr. Deckler in the Personnel Office.
9. Is that door open?
10. He has a wonderful life!

Page 31

Listen to the conversations and put the number under the correct memo.

1. A. I'm afraid he isn't here right now. May I ask who's calling?
   B. Yes. This is Mr. Riley.

2. A. I'm afraid she won't be here until this afternoon.
   B. Please tell her to call William Wiley.

3. A. Do you want to leave a message?
   B. Yes. Please tell her to call Mrs. Tyler.

4. A. Mr. Henderson will be back in a little while.
   B. I see. Please ask him to call his wife.

5. A. They won't be back until sometime on Thursday. Is there a message?
   B. Yes. Please tell them to call Ms. White, their accountant.

Page 33

Listen and choose the correct answer.

1. When is the next flight to Tokyo?
2. How much is the ticket?
3. How much is a round-trip ticket?
4. When does the next bus to Denver leave?
5. When is the next train to Washington?
6. How much is it with the tax?
7. And when is the next plane to Caracas?
8. I'd like a one-way ticket.

Page 41

Listen and choose the word to complete each sentence.

1. You can park between . . .
2. Please cut down that tree in front of . . .
3. They rode their bikes on . . .
4. We live on . . .
5. Don't walk behind . . .
6. They waited for the bus under . . .
7. The train left at . . .
8. He'll put the boxes in . . .
9. Please don't lean against . . .

Page 46

What food items do you hear?

1. A. What do you want me to get at the supermarket?
   B. A quart of milk and a bottle of ketchup.

2. A. Could you get a can of tuna?
   B. All right. Anything else?
   A. No, thank you.

3. A. What do you need from the supermarket?
   B. Let's see. I need a gallon of orange juice and a pound of apples.

4. A. Could you do me a favor?
   B. Sure. What is it?
   A. Could you get half a dozen eggs and a pound of butter?

5. A. We need a loaf of white bread.
   B. Okay. Anything else?
   A. Yes. A box of chocolate chip cookies.

6. A. Let's buy a bag of potato chips.
   B. Okay. Good idea.

7. A. Do we need anything from the supermarket?
   B. Yes. We need a jar of peanut butter.
   A. Okay. Anything else?
   B. Oh, yes. We also need a head of lettuce.

8. A. What should I get at the supermarket?
   B. I think we need some bananas.
   A. Is one bunch enough?
   B. Yes. I think so.

9. A. Could you do me a favor?
   B. Sure. What?
   A. Could you get half a gallon of apple juice at the supermarket?
   B. No problem.

10. A. What do we need at the supermarket?
    B. Why don't you get a pint of vanilla ice cream and a dozen oranges?
    A. Anything else?
    B. No. I think that's all we need.

Page 51

Listen and choose the correct number.

1. That'll be thirteen fifty.
2. Your change is four dollars and five cents.
3. That comes to seventy-two dollars and thirty-six cents.
4. That'll be sixty cents.
5. Your change is twenty-eight dollars.
6. With tax, that comes to ten forty-two.
7. Here's five.
8. That'll be one twenty-five.

Page 55

You will hear four conversations at a restaurant. Put the number next to the correct food items.

Conversation 1

A. What would you like for an appetizer?
B. I'd like a small salad.
A. What would you like as a main dish?
B. I'd like the fried chicken.
A. And would you like anything to drink?
B. Yes. Let me see . . . I'll have a lemonade.

Conversation 2

A. Would you like an appetizer?
B. Yes. I'll have the egg rolls.
A. And for a main dish?
B. I'd like the fish.
A. What would you like to drink?
B. I'll have iced tea, please.

Conversation 3

A. What would you like?
B. For an appetizer, I'd like the mushrooms.
A. All right. What else would you like?

(continued)

B. I'd like the tacos.
A. What would you like to drink?
B. Orange soda, please.

Conversation 4

A. What would you like?
B. I'd like the bread and cheese, the lamb chops, and a glass of mineral water.

Page 57

Listen and choose the correct food.

1. Have a little more.
2. I'd like a few more, please.
3. Please, not too much.
4. Would you like a little more?
5. I already ate too many.
6. Don't give me too much, please.

Page 68

Listen and decide what these people are talking about.

1. I like this one. It's much more powerful than that one.
2. This is too short. You need a longer one.
3. These are much nicer than those.
4. It's much warmer than it was yesterday.
5. I think we should buy this one. It's more comfortable than that one.
6. Buy that one. It's much prettier than this one.
7. Let's buy this one. It's larger and more attractive than that one.
8. Let's buy that one. It's much quieter than this one.
9. I like this one. It's much better than the one across the street.

Page 79

Listen to each conversation and decide which check the people are talking about.

1. A. I forgot to tell you. I wrote a check to University Bookstore.
   B. Do you remember the amount?
   A. Yes. Fifty dollars.

2. A. I'm going to write a check to City University.
   B. Okay. What's the amount?
   A. A hundred and fifty dollars.

3. A. The bill from City Hospital is due next week.
   B. Okay. I'll write the check tomorrow.

4. A. Did you write a check for fifteen dollars to City Bookstore?
   B. Yes.

5. A. How much was the check for?
   B. A hundred and twenty-five dollars.

6. A. Don't forget to write a check to the city for water and trash collection.
   B. Don't worry. I won't forget.

Page 81

Listen to the conversations and choose the correct amount.

1. A. What did you put in?
   B. A quarter.

2. A. What did you lose?
   B. A quarter and a dime.

3. A. How much did you lose?
   B. Two quarters and a dime.

4. A. What did you put in the vending machine?
   B. Two quarters.

5. A. How much did you put in the machine?
   B. A quarter, two dimes, and a nickel.

6. A. I just lost two quarters and three dimes.
   B. That's terrible!

7. A. How much did you put in?
   B. A quarter and two dimes.

8. A. How much change do you have?
   B. Three quarters, a dime, and a nickel.

9. A. How much change do you need?
   B. Two nickels and two dimes.

What numbers do you hear?

1. In most U.S. states, young people can drive on their 16th birthday.
2. My parents just bought a house on 25th Street.
3. Don't forget to pay the telephone bill by December 3rd.
4. Jim had a fantastic party on his 21st birthday.
5. The electric bill is due on October 22nd.
6. We're having a party for our 12th anniversary.
7. I wrote a check to pay the gas bill on March 30th.
8. I deposited my check on the 1st day of the month.
9. The address is twenty forty-five 23rd Street.
10. July 4th is an important holiday.
11. Happy 21st birthday!
12. My new office is on the 70th floor.

Page 89

Listen and write the number under the correct picture.

1. Please mail this letter to Mrs. King.
2. Please give this report to Howard.
3. Please write a memo to the Board of Directors.
4. Please fax this to the Ajax Company.
5. Please read this announcement to all our employees.

Page 93

Listen and decide whether the following statements are true or false.

1. An accurate typist makes a lot of mistakes.
2. A good waiter takes orders carefully.
3. A good actor acts well.
4. A careful painter makes a lot of mistakes.
5. Companies usually like to have neat workers.
6. A graceful dancer isn't a good dancer.

Page 95

Listen and choose the correct word.

1. Juan is an excellent translator. He translates very . . .
2. Diane types extremely . . .
3. My son speaks very politely, but my daughter speaks even . . .
4. You drive very . . .
5. I can't hear the TV. Please make it . . .
6. Uh-oh! There's a police officer. I think you should drive a little . . .

Page 107

Listen and choose the correct sign.

1. A. Are you allowed to camp here?
   B. No, you aren't.

2. A. Are you allowed to smoke cigarettes in this room?
   B. No, you aren't.

3. A. Let's go swimming!
   B. We can't. Look at the sign.

4. A. There's a parking place over there.
   B. No, there isn't. Read that sign.

5. A. Can we go ice skating on this lake?
   B. No, you can't.

6. A. Uh-oh! We can't fish here.
   B. You're right.

Page 109

Listen and decide where each of these conversations is taking place.

1. A. You aren't allowed in there right now. They're operating.
   B. Oh, I didn't know that.

2. A. Please don't bring your drink in here. You might spill it on the books.
   B. Oh. Sorry.

3. A. Please don't stand in front of the white line. It's not safe.
   B. Oh. Thanks for telling me.

4. A. Are you allowed to park here?
   B. Are you a customer?
   A. Yes, I am.
   B. Then you can park here.

5. A. Can I turn right here?
   B. No. The sign at the corner says DO NOT ENTER.

6. A. Are you allowed to fish here?
   B. Certainly

7. A. Excuse me. You aren't allowed to swim here.
   B. Hmm. NO SWIMMING. Thanks for telling me.

8. A. Are you allowed to eat in here?
   B. No, you aren't.

Page 111

Listen to the conversation and choose the correct conclusion.

1. A. Oops!
   B. What's the matter?
   A. Didn't you see the sign?
   B. The sign? What sign? What did it say?
   A. NO U TURN.
   B. Oops!

2. A. Look out! There's a STOP sign!
   B. Oh, my goodness. I didn't see it.

3. A. What's the matter?
   B. Didn't you see that DO NOT ENTER sign?
   A. No. Uh-oh!

4. A. You aren't allowed to make a left turn here.
   B. Really? Are you sure?
   A. Yes. Didn't you see the sign?
   B. Oops!

5. A. Sir, I have to give you a ticket.
   B. Why, Officer?
   A. Didn't you see that sign? It says NO RIGHT TURN ON RED.
   B. Oops!

6. A. I'm afraid you're going to have to turn around.
   B. Why? What's the matter?
   A. This is a ONE WAY street.
   B. Oh, my goodness!

Page 115

Listen to the conversations and put the number next to the rule being broken.

1. A. Where do you want this garbage?
   B. You can just leave it in the hall.

2. A. Can I leave my car in front of the entrance?
   B. I don't think so.
   A. Well, I'll leave it here for just a minute.

3. A. What time is it?
   B. Midnight!
   A. What? I can't hear you! Turn the stereo down!

4. A. Why are you opening the window?
   B. It's going to be cold tonight. I'm bringing in the plants.

5. A. Where are my shirts? Where are the towels?
   B. On the balcony. The dryer is broken.

6. A. Be careful up there!
   B. Okay!

Page 139

Listen and choose the best response.

1. My wife just got a raise!
2. I just lost twenty dollars!
3. Our landlord raised our rent again!
4. My grandfather had a heart attack last week.
5. We just sold our house for a lot of money!
6. I didn't win the lottery!

Listen and put the number under the correct picture.

1. A. Did you hear the news?
   B. No. What happened?
   A. There's going to be a big snowstorm tomorrow.
   B. Really? Where did you hear that?
   A. I heard it on my car radio.

2. A. Did you hear the news?
   B. No. What?
   A. Our apartment building is going to be sold.
   B. Really? Where did you hear that?
   A. The next-door neighbor told me.

3. A. Did you hear the news?
   B. No. What happened?
   A. Our teacher is going to have a baby.
   B. Really? Where did you hear that?
   A. Someone in gym class told me.

4. A. Did you hear the news?
   B. No. What?
   A. The city is having very bad financial problems.
   B. Where did you hear that?
   A. I saw it on the 6:00 news.

5. A. Did you hear the news?
   B. No. What happened?
   A. The zoo is going to close!
   B. No kidding! Where did you hear that?
   A. I read it in today's paper.

6. A. Did you hear the news?
   B. No. What?
   A. The secretary in our department and the supervisor are getting married!
   B. Really? Where did you hear that?
   A. I overheard it on the elevator.

7. A. Did you hear the news?
   B. No. What happened?
   A. The people down the street are getting a divorce!
   B. Really? Where did you hear that?
   A. The mailman told me.

8. A. Did you hear the news?
   B. No. What?
   A. There's going to be a big English test tomorrow!
   B. Are you serious?! Where did you hear that?
   A. Someone told me at lunch.

9. A. Did you hear the news?
   B. No. What?
   A. You're going to be promoted!
   B. I am?! Where did you hear that?
   A. The boss whispered it to me . . . but you aren't supposed to know yet!

Listen and choose the word you hear.

1. Mr. Hale is on the phone.
2. The meeting is on Sunday.
3. Excuse me. Your brother is here to see you.
4. Oh, no! We're out of ice!
5. Our neighbors are making a lot of noise!
6. It's really cold in this restaurant. I hope they turn up the heat!
7. I'm sorry. The escalator is out of order.
8. Excuse me. Where's the chicken?

Listen and choose the correct response.

1. Mr. Wilkins was in a great mood today.
2. It won't break down.
3. They're going to do their homework together.
4. We have to get back to work.
5. She gets excellent grades.
6. Bob and Bill went home early.
7. It's going to be a difficult test.
8. The doctor wasn't very busy.
9. She quit.

Listen and decide where each conversation is taking place.

1. A. I'd like to know the balance of my checking account.
   B. Certainly. What's your account number?

2. A. I need an X-ray of your gums.
   B. All right. Can you do it right now?

3. A. You just missed the exit!
   B. Uh-oh! I'll get off at the next one.

4. A. I just lost two quarters!
   B. Which machine did you put your clothes in?

5. A. I'd like a refund, please.
   B. Could I see your receipt?

6. A. Did you push the button?
   B. Yes. But it won't start.

7. A. We're overbooked tonight.
   B. Oh, no! What are we going to do?

8. A. What happened?
   B. I burned myself on the stove.
   A. Okay. Take a seat. The nurse will see you soon.

9. A. Do you have a strong cold medicine?
   B. Yes, I do. Try this.

Do the speakers agree or disagree?

1. A. The news program on Channel 4 is the best.
   B. I agree. It really is.

2. A. Arnold should be promoted.
   B. I disagree.

3. A. John Miller will be an excellent mayor.
   B. I'm not so sure. I think he needs more experience.

4. A. Karen works very hard. You should be proud of her.
   B. We are.

5. A. That's excellent news!
   B. It certainly is.

6. A. I think we'll get our security deposit back.
   B. I don't.

7. A. I think Norman should quit.
   B. You're right.

8. A. I think we should be going now.
   B. But we just got here!

9. A. This was a delicious lunch.
   B. It was?!

GRAMMAR INDEX

A

Able to, **96-98**
Adjectives, **56, 66-73, 92, 93, 142, 143, 160, 161**
Adverbs, **92, 93**

C

Can, **6-9**
Comparative of Adverbs, **94, 95**
Comparatives, **66-69, 134**
Could, **10, 11, 22, 23, 97, 98, 102**
Count/Non-Count Nouns, **56, 57, 60**

F

Future: Going to, **74, 75, 116, 117, 138-141, 144, 145**
Future: Will, **28-31, 100, 101, 116, 117, 144, 145**
Future Continuous Tense, **136, 137**

H

Have Got to, **156-159**
Have to, **74, 75, 96, 156-159**

I

Imperatives, **22-25, 36, 37, 58-60, 76, 77, 100, 101**
Impersonal Expressions with "You", **106-109, 114, 115**
Indirect Objects, **10, 11, 88, 89**

M

May, **28, 29, 31, 48, 52**
Might, **144, 145**
Must, **118, 119**

O

Object Pronouns, **10, 11, 29**

Ordinal Numbers, **82, 83**
Ought to, **120, 121**

P

Partitives, **44-49, 52-55, 58-60**
Past Continuous Tense, **112, 113**
Past Tense, **12, 13, 35, 36, 38, 39, 80, 81, 100, 101, 112, 113, 150, 151**
Possessive Adjectives, **10, 129**
Possessive Nouns, **128, 134, 135**
Possessive Pronouns, **134, 135**
Prepositions of Location, **36-39**
Present Continuous Tense, **14**
Pronoun Review, **128, 129**

R

Reflexive Pronouns, **100, 101**

S

Short Answers, **132, 133**
Should, **14, 15, 74, 75, 80, 81, 94, 120, 121, 152, 153, 158, 159**
Simple Present Tense, **2-5, 14, 15, 130, 131**
Superlatives, **70-73**

T

This/That/These/Those, **60-68**
Time Expressions, **16, 17, 28-34, 74, 75, 156, 157**
Two-Word Verbs, **8, 9**

W

Want to, **26, 27**
WH-Questions, **2-5, 26, 27, 142, 143**
Would, **54-57**

Y

Yes/No Questions, **4, 5**

TOPIC INDEX